The Beginner's Guide to eating disorders recovery

Nancy J. Kolodny, MA, MSW, LCSW

gürze books

The Beginner's Guide to Eating Disorders Recovery
©2004 Nancy J. Kolodny

Gürze Books
PO Box 2238
Carlsbad, CA 92018
(800) 756-7533
www.gurze.com

Front cover design Abacus Graphics, Oceanside, CA

The author and publisher of this book intend for this publication to provide accurate information. It is sold with the understanding that it is meant to complement, not substitute for, professional medical and/or psychological services.

The individuals described in this book have been thoroughly disguised to preserve confidentiality.

Portions of this book were originally published in *When Food's a Foe* by Nancy Kolodny (Little, Brown and Company, 1998).

The author is grateful to the following for permission to reprint previously published material:
    "The Eating Attitudes Text: An Index of the Symptoms of Anorexia Nervosa," by David M. Garner and Paul E. Garfinkel, Psychological Medicine 9:278 (1979). Reprinted with the permission of Cambridge University Press. EAT-26 by David M. Garner (1982).
    Definitions from the DSM-IV-TR reprinted with permission from the Diagnostic and Statistical Manual of Mental Disorders, Fourth Edition, Text Revision. Washington, DC, American Psychiatric Association, 2000.
    "Food Guide Pyramid" reprinted courtesy of the U.S. Department of Agriculture/ U.S. Department of Health and Human Services.

Library of Congress Cataloging-in-Publication Data

Kolodny, Nancy J.
   The beginner's guide to eating disorders recovery / Nancy J. Kolodny.
      p. cm.
   Summary: Provides information on anorexia and bulimia, and discusses what is involved in recovering from eating disorders.
   Includes bibliographical references.
   ISBN 0-936077-45-X (alk. paper)
   1. Eating disorders--Juvenile literature. 2. Eating disorders--Treatment--Juvenile literature. [1. Anorexia nervosa. 2. Bulimia. 3. Eating disorders.] I. Title.
   RC552.E18K648 2003
   616.85'26--dc22

                              2003018480

1 3 5 7 9 0 8 6 4 2

This book is dedicated with love to my family and with gratitude to the many people struggling with eating disorders who have allowed me to work with them and learn from them.

contents

Journey of Recovery

by Christie C., age 20

I want you to notice I've straightened my hair
That I did my eye makeup different than before
I want you to notice that I have a new strut in my walk, edge in
*   my voice*
I want you to notice the circles under my eyes
I want you to know that it's not mascara
I want you to notice that I bit all of my nails off – they were
*   breaking anyway*
I want you to see my foot tapping
And it's not in time with the music
I want you to see my pale skin
I want you to realize it's not that gray – not usually
I want you to see my fingers shaking wildly and my eyes glazed
*   open*
I want you to know it's from the diet pills I took today; six of
*   them*
I want you to know I tried to stop taking them, but couldn't get
*   up the next day*
I want you to know my arm needs a Bandaid
It started to bleed after I poked at it too much
I want you to know that I can feel my heart
That it basically jumps into my hand with every pulse
I want you to know that my heart hurts; both of them do
I want you to know what it feels like to feel everything draining
*   down my throat*

To have chest pains that paralyze me
I want you to know that I lie awake at night, terrified that if I
    actually fall asleep, I won't wake up again
I want you to know that I didn't sleep the whole week before I
    came home
Boys wrote me poems and I drank with them and kissed them
I want you to know that it wasn't really me
I want you to know that I thought it would make me feel beautiful
It didn't
I want you to know that I hate my current self
I want you to know that I'd rather crawl in a hole than live right
    now
I want you to know that I'm trying so hard
So hard, I want to poke at my own skin, poke with nubby finger-
    nails
I want you to know that I'm stuck
I want you to know that I want out of this pit, but I'm so dread-
    fully stuck
I want you to take my life from my hands
I want you to see that I'm a mess
That I've broken into about a million pieces
I want you to see that I'm not stable
I want you to notice that when I stand up too fast, I grab onto a
    stationary object
I want you to know that's because I feel dizzy
My head rushes
I can't feel my feet
Everything goes black
I want you to know what the nutritionist told me
She told me I'm dying
That I'm experiencing pre-heart-attack symptoms
I want you to know how terribly that scared me
I couldn't tell anyone until now
I didn't want to tell myself
Because I still can't stop
I want you to know that she said my next workout could be my last
I want you to know that everyone knows me at the gym

I want you to know that I went anyway, even when I felt inside I was dying

I want you to realize that I went because I would feel like a failure if I didn't

I ended up feeling like a failure anyway

I want you to know that I'm sorry

I want you to help me find a new me

Or at least get the old me back

I want you to fix me

I want you to notice what's been fixed

I want you to notice that I finally don't slurp when I drink

That I can hold a fork better than anyone

That I make no sounds when I chew

I want you to observe the adult I've become

The child I still am

I want you

I want you to know that I need help

That I need you

I want you to make decisions for me right now because I can't

I want you to hug that scary part of me

That's all I ever really wanted

I'm scared

I'm lost

I need help

I changed a lot while you were away

I just wanted to let you know

introduction

I began my working life as a high school English teacher. As the years went by, I noticed that many of my students were struggling with the challenges of growing up. They wanted someone to talk to about their lives and the problems they were facing, and needed more emotional support and direction than I could give them in my role as a teacher. So, I decided to switch careers and learn to be that kind of listener.

I became a therapist in 1980. In 1981, I was hired by a psychiatrist who was beginning a self-help program for people with eating disorders. I was immediately struck by the intensity, intelligence, and complexity of his patients and felt that this was the group of people I wanted to work with for the rest of my professional life. And that's what I've done.

People often find it odd that I seem to "get" what eating disorders are all about and ask me if I have had one. The answer is "no." However, I *am* a mother of three now-grown daughters. During their high school and college years, each of them had close friendships with young people who were struggling with their eating and weight.

In fact, one of my children was the tenth-grade boarding-school roommate of Marya Hornbacher, the author of *Wasted: A Memoir of Anorexia and Bulimia*. I mention this because their relationship is described in some detail in Marya's book. It was difficult for me, as a parent, to see my own daughter struggle on a very intense and personal level to help her friend. It also made me sad and sometimes angry that I couldn't fly out to Michigan from my home in Connecticut to take over and "fix" things for them.

For this reason, I became much more sensitive than I might otherwise have been to the frustrations many parents feel when they can't just jump in and "fix" things for their loved ones. It also gave me great respect for the role of a relative (or friend) in the recovery process. I hope that respect shines through in this book.

The Beginner's Guide to Eating Disorders Recovery is designed to give you a clear and complete picture of what it's like to have an eating disorder and what is involved in recovering from one. It is written with teenagers and young adults in mind, but it will also be helpful for anyone who wants to understand the basics about eating disorders. It couples the wisdom gleaned from years of listening to clients' stories with the latest information and research about the disorders themselves and the people who struggle with them.

Think of me as a teacher giving you a curriculum about anorexia and bulimia, with this book as the syllabus. In addition to the factual information, you'll discover when, why, and how to examine and evaluate eating-disordered behaving and thinking—whether your own or someone else's.

My intention is to reveal (and honor) the logic that underlies and supports an eating disorder. I want to provide you with the facts and demystify what really happens behind the surface of these devastating illnesses. To this end, I have included graphic descriptions that might make you a bit queasy, or surprise and even shock you. *My objective is not to teach you how to mimic the self-destructive things some anorexics and bulimics do. On the contrary.* My hope is that you will recognize the extremely dangerous potential of eating disorders and will not use this book as a way to add "tricks" to your own repertoire of self-harming behaviors.

I then go into "challenge mode" and describe what *has* to happen for that logic to be replaced with *non-eating-disordered* thinking and behaving. So, as a beginner's guide, this book will answer the following kinds of questions:

- What are eating disorders?

- How does an eating disorder start?

- How does an eating disorder affect someone's daily life?

- Why does one person develop anorexia and another develop bulimia?

- Does an eating disorder serve any purpose?

- When does an eating disorder become a serious problem?

- Is recovery possible?

- Can an eating disorder be prevented?

- How does therapy help and what kind of therapy is useful?

- Who should be involved in the therapy process?

- How much input and authority does the eating-disordered person have regarding treatment decisions?

- What are the benefits of therapy and recovery? Do they outweigh the effort it takes to recover?

If you know for sure that you have an eating disorder and are presently struggling with anorexia and/or bulimia, the strategies and information in *The Beginner's Guide* will address any ambivalence you may have about recovery and give you practical ideas for what steps to take. It will challenge you to think, ask you to do some work, and help you to be honest with yourself and the people you care about (and who care about you). It will give you tools to regain some of the control you may feel is missing in your life. In addition, it will encourage you to make choices for constructive change so you can let go of an eating disorder safely, gradually, consciously, and willingly.

If you believe you might be on the verge of developing a full-blown eating disorder, *The Beginner's Guide* will show you how to examine your present system of values, attitudes, and beliefs, pay attention to your communication style, see what works, change what doesn't, and increase the odds that the eating disorder won't creep into or take over your life.

If you are a relative, friend, or coworker of someone who has anorexia or bulimia, *The Beginner's Guide* will help you understand the complexities of the person's thoughts and behaviors, their daily struggles, how you fit into those struggles, and how you can voice your concerns and frustrations without contributing to the problem.

Try to read *The Beginner's Guide* from this Introduction through the last chapter without skipping around, because each chapter builds upon information offered previously. Part One explains basic facts about eating disorders, with a focus on anorexia and bulimia, the connection between body-image and self-esteem, and when habits become obsessions, compulsions, or addictions. Part Two discusses the recovery process, with chapters on initial steps and "Coming Out" (admitting there is a problem). Several chapters explore how to choose a therapist, what to expect in therapy, and the most current information on medication options. Specific strategies for overcoming eating disorders are offered in two chapters entitled "First Steps in Recovery" and "Sustaining Recovery." A final chapter offers specific advice for loved ones.

If you are struggling with an eating disorder yourself, do the written exercises throughout and keep track of your responses in a journal or notebook as you read and react. By the time you have gone through the whole book, you will be much more self-aware than when you started. You will have a clear idea of what eating disorders do to and for you (or someone else). But most important of all, you will learn to be proud of the positive changes you make for yourself as you travel the road to recovery. And who knows? In the end, your knowledge and experience might prevent an eating disorder from creeping into someone else's life!

PART I

Eating Disorders Explained

chapter one

A Quick Peek at Eating Disorders

"Why can't you just eat like a normal person?"
— Mother of a 19-year-old anorexic

Do you know what it means to be hungry and how it feels to satisfy hunger? Are you aware of your food preferences and do you pay attention to them? Do you understand nutrition without being obsessive about it? Can you overeat or miss a meal, and not feel anxious? Is eating a comfortable and important part of your social life? Do you take food and the actual process of eating for granted? If so, you're fortunate.

Millions of people aren't so lucky. Their thoughts and behaviors about food, eating, self-image, and self-worth have become illogical, out-of-control, and so intense that they develop actual medical conditions that are referred to as eating disorders. This book focuses on anorexia nervosa and bulimia nervosa, two of the most common types of eating disorders.

When YOU Have an Eating Disorder

When you have an eating disorder, you don't think about or use food the way the majority of us do. Instead of eating when you're hungry, eating for nutrition and good health, eating for pleasure, or eating to share good times with others, you have an unusual relationship with food. You do things that may seem bizarre, such as performing odd rituals before you eat, or vomiting or taking laxatives to get rid of the food you have eaten. You may be so obsessed that eating, or not eating, becomes physically and emotionally destructive. In fact, an eating disorder can feel (and be) like having an addiction—very difficult to stop once the habits and rituals have become ingrained.

As this focus on food and eating dominates your daily routines, family and friends usually become involved and get caught on an emotional roller coaster that is hard for everyone to cope with and even harder for them to understand. They see changes in you; you deny the changes. They want to talk about what's happening; you don't. They think it's about food and eating; you may realize it's about more than what is obvious, but choose to keep that hidden. Mealtimes become occasions for conflict, emotional distress, and physical discomfort. The dining table turns into a battleground where wars are fought—between people and even inside your head. It's virtually impossible to sit down, eat, and enjoy the experience.

If you can't, or won't, get yourself out of this self-destructive cycle or don't get help to break its grip, you will endure potentially serious consequences. Your body can suffer irreversible damage. Your soul will feel starved. Psychologically, you may feel profoundly depressed, lose a lot of self-esteem, and even become suicidal.

Anorexia and Bulimia Defined

What are these disorders?

- Anorexia nervosa: a self-starvation disorder. The anorexic (the person afflicted with anorexia) ignores hunger, restricts the amounts and kinds of food eaten to such an extent that starvation is a very real possibility—as is death.

- Bulimia nervosa: a binge-purge disorder. The bulimic

(the person afflicted with bulimia) gorges (binges) on enormous amounts of food—sometimes thousands of calories at one time—and then gets rid of it (purges) by vomiting, excessive use of laxatives, or other means. Bulimia is also dangerous to a person's physical and mental health.

Some people flip back and forth between bulimia and anorexia, bingeing for a while, then restricting, and resorting to bingeing again. There is much variety in people's patterns and why the patterns occur.

Who Gets These Disorders?

Virtually anyone can develop an eating disorder—people of all ages, from all walks of life, and all ethnic and socioeconomic groups.

> **Eating disorders can touch you if you live on a farm or on Fifth Avenue, if you grew up in a ghetto or in a mansion. Eating disorders don't discriminate.**

Females are victims more often than males, but young men are showing up for treatment in ever-increasing numbers. This fact may be related to increased societal awareness, better diagnostic tools available to health care providers, and the understanding that eating disorders are nothing to be ashamed of.

Statistics about who is affected by eating disorders vary depending upon the source of the data and the nature of the research. In general, the following numbers tell a chilling, story:

- Conservative estimates indicate that after puberty, between 5 and 10 million females and 1 million males struggle with eating disorders (Eating Disorder Referral and Information Center, *www.edreferral.com*)

The age of onset varies (Anorexia Nervosa and Associated Disorders, *www.anad.org/facts.html*):

- 86% of people with eating disorders report onset by age 20;

- 43% of people with eating disorders report onset between ages 16and 20;

- 33% of people with eating disorders report onset between ages 11 and 15;

- 10% report onset at age 10 or younger.

What Causes an Eating Disorder?

Eating disorders don't just "happen" or pop up out of nowhere. They start for a variety of reasons, which are ultimately personal and unique to each individual. They can be triggered by something as innocent a desire to be "in" with friends who are dieting to achieve a certain goal; for example, "looking good" in bikinis for a trip to the beach. They might be triggered by a need to be accepted by a crowd of kids who are focused on weight and shape and have a "group speak" that puts down anyone who doesn't fit their thin ideal. In some susceptible individuals, eating disorders can be triggered by a romantic break-up, family crisis, a problem in school, or the stress of leaving home for the first time. Even one derogatory comment about their appearance from a parent, teacher, friend or coach can propel a susceptible and vulnerable young person into anorexic or bulimic behaviors.

In its initial stages, an eating disorder might seem to be a useful tool for handling life's challenges. It might provide a way to cope with problems that you can't otherwise openly discuss, confront, or manage within your family or network of relationships. You might find that it helps you feel powerful in some areas of life and makes up for low self-esteem in others.

> **An eating disorder "talks" when words fail.**

In reality, an eating disorder is a symptom, a signal that something is wrong in a person's life. And because an eating disorder usually masks what really needs to be corrected, it is ultimately a self-destructive strategy.

Are Eating Disorders Serious?

Eating disorders are very serious. Anorexia and bulimia will eventually create problems in every aspect of your life: physical, emotional, social, intellectual, even economic. Eating disorders can last for as little as one year or less, to decades or more. They usually get progressively worse unless they are faced and treated. In long-term situations, the intensity of the disorder can vary along a continuum from debilitating, life-threatening symptoms to mildly annoying ones that are not life-threatening per se, but negatively impact your quality of life.

In the most severe cases, death is a real possibility. The mortality rate among people with anorexia is 0.56% per year, "which is about 12 times higher than the annual death rate due to all causes of death among females ages 15-24 in the general population," according to the National Institute for Mental Health (NIMH) (*www.nimh.nih.gov/ publicat/eatingdisorder.cfm*). The ANRED website (Anorexia Nervosa and Related Eating Disorders, Inc., (*www.anred.com/stats.html*) reports that without treatment, 20% of people with serious eating disorders will die; with treatment, the number drops to between 2 and 3%.

When an eating disorder is in its early stages and the thoughts and behaviors are relatively easy to hide from others, you can fool yourself and the people around you by downplaying its seriousness. You can act as if what you're doing is socially acceptable and totally normal. But later on, once you're "into" the disorder, the seriousness of your situation becomes clear, especially when it's time to stop either the dieting, bingeing, or the binge-purge pattern. Some people can't stop because they are mentally and physically addicted to their disorders. Others don't want to stop and resist treatment to help them do so. The reasons for this are complicated and will be discussed throughout this book. But whatever the reasons people have for becoming eating disordered, the results can be disastrous to physical and mental health, to family harmony, to friendships and relationships, to school or work performance, and to self-esteem.

Is There A Cure?

Diagnosing and correcting an eating disorder isn't as straight-forward as diagnosing a medical condition like measles or chicken pox, where a doctor knows what causes the illness, how long it will last, and the best course of treatment. There are no immunizations to protect someone from getting an eating disorder. However, people who are susceptible tend to have similar kinds of family histories, share certain personality traits with other anorexics and bulimics, and have symptoms in common.

An eating disorder can be overcome, but the process isn't easy. You have to be willing to get better and put in the time and effort needed to make that happen. You have to take risks, trust in other people, be honest, and challenge some of your beliefs. Ultimately, recovery will take you on a "journey into self" that will be illuminating, occasionally humorous, often poignant, sometimes difficult and painful, and always worthwhile.

What about Prevention?

Prevention is possible, too, and the best preventive strategy is to become educated. If you're willing to read about anorexia and bulimia and talk to people who have struggled with the disorders, you'll understand the thought processes, self-talk, and behaviors that might make you vulnerable. If you're already trapped, educating yourself can help you cope with and heal any mental or physical damage that you might have done to yourself.

Factual knowledge clarifies what is happening and provides

direction and strategies to change dangerous situations. It also gives you a reasonable expectation that you will succeed.

That's the purpose of this book: to give you the tools for success in the face of a difficult challenge.

Ten Basic Facts
about Eating Disorders

1. People with eating disorders think about and use food in ways that are different from others.

2. For someone with an eating disorder, eating or not eating becomes physically and emotionally destructive.

3. An eating disorder changes relationships with friends and family as the focus on food and eating increases.

4. Eating disorders don't discriminate. They affect people of all ages, both sexes, from all walks of life, and all ethnic and socioeconomic groups.

5. After puberty, between 5 and 10 million females and 1 million males struggle with eating disorders; 43% of them report onset between ages 16 and 20; 33% between ages 11 and 15.

6. An eating disorder can last from less than a year to decades or more.

7. Eating disorders don't just "happen" or pop up out of nowhere. They have logic, initially serve a purpose in your life, and may be triggered by a specific life event.

8. Eating disorders can be dangerous if left to develop unchecked. They will create serious problems in every aspect of life: physical, emotional, social, intellectual, economic. They can be fatal.

9. Recovery is possible by challenging the beliefs and changing the behaviors that support the eating disorder.

10. The first step in preventing eating disorders is to become educated about them.

chapter two

Self-Image, Body-Image, and the Struggle for Self-Esteem

"I found out I was voted "prettiest" the day we got our senior year-books. When I looked at my photo on that page, all I could focus on was that my nose was too broad, my lips uneven, and one of my eyebrows was thicker than the other. I didn't feel like I deserved the vote."

— Amy J., age 17

Do you agree with any of the following statements? "I have a pretty good sense of where I am in life and where I'm headed." "I'm a work in progress and I'm okay with the unknowns right now. They're kind of exciting." "My body is fine just as it is." "I accept myself no matter what I look like." "I'm honestly satisfied with who I am." "I like myself!" "I like me for me!"

If so, chances are good that your *self-image* (your sense of identity) is secure, your *body-image* (what you see when you look in the mirror and how comfortable or satisfied you are with your size, shape, and appearance) is healthy, and your *self-esteem* (the feelings you have about yourself) is high.

People who can't agree with any of those self-statements tend to be hard on themselves and share the following traits:

- they're not self-accepting;
- they barely like who they are;
- they often feel like "losers";
- They *really* believe the cultural myth that thinness is necessary to be taken seriously, to have any social clout, to "fit in."

We happen to live in a weight-conscious, fashion-conscious, diet-conscious society that puts a premium on good looks, is intolerant of physical imperfection, and implies that people who are thin are somehow smarter, luckier, more interesting than, and generally superior to, those who aren't. So it's not exactly unreasonable that someone would want to be thin.

But focusing too much on trying to achieve that "look" can be so physically and psychologically draining that it is difficult to accomplish much else of importance, such as learning about yourself, exploring and developing skills and talents, and connecting with others.

Chain Links

What exactly are *self-image, body-image,* and *self-esteem* and how are they related? They are three elements of self-perception which, like chain links, can exist independently of one another, but are stronger when connected together. People who struggle with these elements of self-perception are vulnerable to eating disorders. Why? Read on.

Self-Image: The First Chain Link

Self-image is your sense of who you are and who you want to become—your identity. Self-image can change frequently because of the many influences and pressures that shape it, such as: your values and beliefs, your parents' hopes and expectations for you, the impact of friends' opinions, jobs you may have, fads and fashions, people you admire, the things you learn in school, and what you learn about yourself as you grow up. It takes time to develop a "user-friendly" self-image that makes you feel balanced and content. Until then, you're susceptible to lots of emotional ups and downs as you react to these influences and pressures, adjust, and try to find a comfortable match between the external pressures and your private, internal ones.

Body-Image: The Second Chain Link

A big part of *self-image* is connected to *body-image*: how comfortable and satisfied you are with the size, shape, and appearance of your body. Body-image is changeable and has some peculiar characteristics:

- *What you see when you look in a mirror may be different from what others see when they look at you.* You may see flaws and think you're a mess, while someone else may think you look absolutely great.

- *Body-image can be inaccurate; what you think you see may not be real.* Anorexics, for example, see extra fat on their bodies where none exists.

- *Your mood can affect your body-image and vice versa.* If you're feeling happy, your body-image may seem just fine to you; if you're sad, stressed, or tired, you may feel like there's nothing right about the image you're seeing in the mirror. This change can happen in an instant.

- *Your ideal body-image (how you'd look if you could make yourself "perfect") can clash with the reality of what you see in the mirror.*

As with self-image, body-image develops over time and changes as you move and grow through adolescence. It's primarily influenced by the "three P's": *Parents, Peers,* and the *Press.* Eventually, bits and pieces of several images are incorporated into something unique that feels right and captures the essence of who you are at that moment—a look that fits.

Self-Esteem: The Third Chain Link

Self-esteem, or the feelings you have about yourself, is linked to both your *body-image* and *self-image*. If you can't look the way you think you're supposed to—no matter how hard you try or want to—your ideal and actual body-images clash and you become vulnerable to self-doubts and feelings of inadequacy. Your self-esteem goes down. You lose sight of your positive qualities, miscalculate how you're coming across to others, and misinterpret their reactions to you.

Low self-esteem is one of the conditions that allow an eating disorder into a person's life. Under the best of circumstances, self-esteem can be hard to come by during adolescence—a time filled with emotions.

If you:

- keep your emotions to yourself,
- doubt the validity of the emotions you're experiencing,
- question your right to have such feelings,
- feel afraid to have feelings,
- wonder or say, "Who could like/love me?" or "I don't deserve to be liked/loved,"

chances are your self-esteem is low. That makes it hard to express and acknowledge feelings, another risk factor for developing eating disorders.

You can see that self-esteem is based on a variety of different elements, such as: liking yourself, having a body-image you can appreciate (even if it's not model "perfect"), being able to take some risks in life and not be overwhelmed at the thought of failure, giving yourself credit when you deserve it, and having a realistic self-image based on fact rather than fantasy. When these important elements are present, the thought processes that lead to eating disorders will have less of a chance to invade your mind and take over your life.

When the Chain is Broken: Jeri and Nancy

As we've seen, if you're dissatisfied with your body-image, both your self-image and self-esteem will suffer. And when you don't have high self-esteem, it can be difficult to give yourself honest credit for your accomplishments. You may begin to think of yourself as a loser or a fake, when someone more objective would say that's not so, as in the following example:

> I've always wanted to be popular. I don't enjoy being known as a brain, but I'm shy, normally, so I find it hard to make friends. I know if I were thinner people would like me more; at least they'd take a look at me and see I fit the image of the in-group up here. Then maybe they'd forget that my SAT scores led the school. The way I look right now, I don't think I'd want to be my friend if I were someone else. I'm going on a strict diet today.
>
> – Jeri P., age 17

> I can't tell you how many times Jeri and I have discussed what she just said to you. None of us put her down for being smart; she just can't give herself credit for it. She never believes us when we congratulate her for things like awards she gets at school. She thinks we're making fun. She's never happy with herself. And she has a few really good friends. I know a lot of girls with a zillion acquaintances and no friends they can really trust. I wish Jeri could realize there's a difference between friends for show and friends for real. I'm worried about her.
>
> – Nancy D., age 17, Jeri's best friend

Jeri is a perfect example of someone who sees herself one way while other people see her differently. Her intelligence doesn't seem to give her good feelings or enhance her self-esteem. Jeri undervalues herself so much that she says if she were another person she

wouldn't want to be her friend, and thinks that being thin, i.e. changing her physical self, will make everyone like her or at least give her
a better chance to make friends. She devalues her best talents and
accomplishments and emphasizes the negatives: her shyness and
weight.

Nancy's opinion of Jeri would seem to suggest that Jeri's self-
image isn't close to being accurate. Nancy makes it clear that Jeri
not only has friends, but they're the kind of friends other kids would
love to have: trustworthy confidants. She also says that the kids in
school *do* give Jeri points for being intelligent. Jeri is the one who
puts herself down for that.

What's going on, then? Jeri's self-image is distorted and leaves no
room for self-esteem. She's unhappy with her body-image and over-
emphasizes her physical shortcomings. She underrates her emotional
and intellectual strengths. She has bought into the cultural "thin is
in" bias, so the solution she dreams up for changing her life is to
diet and get thin. (Dieting, however, won't address the question of
why she can't give herself credit or take credit for the other great
things about herself.) Jeri's self-image is distorted and at odds with
what her peers say they really feel about her. It's as if she's wearing
an invisible radio headset locked into a frequency that constantly
transmits negative messages directly to her brain while it scrambles
and obscures anything positive she might be able to hear, think, or
feel about herself.

So, Jeri and people like her are vulnerable to developing eating
disorders because, in general, they tend to pay attention to cultural
and interpersonal "cues" in a very selective way. They heed the ones
that support negative self-evaluation and ignore or discount the ones
that would help them see their positive qualities.

How "Ideal" and Weight Got Linked

You may not realize that the standards defining the cultural
"ideal" are changeable, but they are. In fact, the term "ideal weight"

was first coined when the insurance industry came up with a height-weight table in 1897 that was meant to gauge mortality risk (Gaesser, p. 39). There were no uniform weight charts or guidelines until 1942. At that time, women ages 25 and up who were 5'6" were expected to weigh between 130 and 140 pounds. By 1959, that range dropped to 124-139 pounds (*www.nationaleatingdisorders.org, 2002*). In 1985, new federal guidelines changed the values again and proposed that 18 to 25-year-old women should weigh between 118 and 150 pounds (*U.S. News & World Report*, 1/6/96, p. 54).

"Body Angst" — Why Is THIN So Important?

In our society, the media (TV, radio, movies, newspapers, magazines, the Internet) consistently promote the notion that physical perfection is important and that appearance somehow defines each of us as people. The current "ideal" female form is depicted as a thin body, curve-enhanced (often with breast implants) at the bust level, curve-free or minimally curved at the waist, with a taut abdomen, and slim hips and thighs (often achieved through liposuction). This ideal is far from reality:

> **The average American model is 5'11" tall and weighs 117 pounds but the average American woman is 5'4" tall and weighs 140 pounds!**

These days, most fashion models are thinner than 98% of American women. Even the average store window mannequin wears a size four (Gayle, p. 1)!

It's no wonder, then, that girls and women are dissatisfied with their appearance. In fact, this desire for thinness translates into weight control as big business; so big, that Americans spend approximately 40 billion dollars on diets, dieting, weight-loss products, and health club memberships every year.

Every year something new appears to lure us in. Now, we are encouraged by advertisers to buy bottled waters that are "enhanced" to make them seem "healthier," nutritional supplement bars that are sex-specific to allegedly meet the different dietary needs of males and females. The dollar amount we spend on these, and similar products, has rocketed upwards of 7 billion dollars since 1996!

In the summer of 2002, America Online (AOL) conducted a "body angst" survey that asked, "What do you think is responsible for many women's poor self-image?" Sixty-six percent of the respondents said "impossibly beautiful media images." Other surveys that collect information about dieting behaviors and weight consciousness show that girls and women remain consistently obsessive in their responses from poll to poll and year to year. Now, sadly, these surveys show that girls are becoming obsessed at younger and younger ages. Let's look at some current data from the National Eating Disorders Association:

- 80% of American women are dissatisfied with their appearance;

- 91% of young women surveyed on a college campus had dieted; 22% dieted "often" or "always."

- 42% of first through third grade girls want to be thinner.

- 51% of 9 and 10-year-old girls feel better about themselves if they are on a diet.

- 46% of 9 to 11-year-olds are "sometimes" or "very often" on diets, and of these children, 82% of their families are "sometimes" or "very often" on diets.

Faking it and the Courage to Be "Real"

Interestingly, the people who represent these ideal images rarely look "ideal" in real life. Very often what we see is illusion, through photo retouching and computer enhancement tricks, but we tend to forget that when we try to imitate them. Some movie stars even have body doubles for the nude or semi-nude movie scenes, as Julia Roberts did in "Pretty Woman" (*People*, 6/3/96, p. 68). Others have had extensive plastic surgery to give them the bodies so many of us think we want. Male stars like Tom Cruise and Sylvester Stallone are actually much shorter than they look in the movies, but camera angles are carefully chosen to make them look taller.

Now think about fashion models. If you've ever seen a "before and after" makeover in a magazine, you know how much of a role faking it plays in the whole beauty business. In a *New York Times* article titled, "The Man Who Makes the Pictures Perfect,"(February 2, 2003) Pascal Dangin, the digital retoucher for fashion magazine photographers, explains his work, "Basically, we're selling a product—we're selling an image. To those who say too much retouching, I say you are bogus. This is the world that we're living in. Everything is glorified. I say live in your time."

In a courageous stand that counters the prevailing impression about her physical attributes, Jamie Lee Curtis allowed *More* magazine (September 2002) to publish an unretouched photo of her that was featured online. She did it so that the public would realize that her glamorous image and reputation for having a great figure is, in her words, "a fraud."

Another courageous decision was made in 2002 by the Editor-in-Chief of *YM*—a "No Diet" policy: they would no longer publish articles that would intensify and/or support the weight-obsessed focus of so many young teen readers. And they feature models of all sizes!

Weight Prejudice: The Fear of Fat

The flip side of glorifying thinness is degrading fat, which results in a cultural phenomenon called "weight prejudice." Being thin is associated with many good qualities such as being smart, social, successful, restrained, loveable; being fat is associated with the opposite qualities such as being dull, antisocial, a failure, having no willpower, and being unlovable.

As a culture, unfortunately, we have come to accept these stereotypes and judge people accordingly. This causes millions of individuals to strive for thinness at any cost, and fear being fat more than any other condition. Over 50% of females ages 18-25 "would prefer to be run over by a truck than be fat," and two-thirds of those surveyed "would rather be mean or stupid" than fat! (*The Alliance for Eating Disorder Awareness, www.eatingdisorderinfo.org*)

The fact is, though, that weight is, to a large degree, dependent on heredity, and it is possible to be both "fat" and "fit." Statistically, the people with thin bodies aren't the healthiest, don't live the longest, aren't happier or more successful or more loved than people with large bodies. And it's incorrect to assume that heavy people have poor diets and don't exercise.

It's also wrong to assume that *all* heavy people will eventually suffer from the physical complications of obesity such as arthritis, type 2 diabetes, or high blood pressure. Some will, some won't. Recent research cited in *Shape* magazine (January, 2004, pp. 66-67) supports the idea that *fitness* (how efficiently your cardiovascular system delivers oxygen to your muscles) is a more reliable predictor of your health and longevity than are your weight or fat (as measured by your BMI [body mass index]).

> **You can't judge a book by its cover;
> a big body can be a healthy one!**

You don't have to be a super-sleuth to find glaring examples of an antifat bias. It's subtle and it's everywhere. Fat people are often overlooked for jobs or romance, are usually negatively stereotyped, may have a harder time getting health or life insurance, and are routinely faced with blatant rudeness.

In the media, men often rag on the condition of women's bodies. Turn on a shock jock like Howard Stern and you hear the bias running throughout the show for hours a day. Reality TV contestants generally look like they could have stepped off the pages of fashion magazines. Even in the one exception, "Average Joe," male contestants vying to become the love interest of the woman contestant were secretly taped talking about and demeaning the appearance of her heavyset "cousin." Later, in a classic "gotcha!" moment, they discovered the "cousin" was actually the female contestant in disguise that made her *look* obese.

Clearly, the bias can be directed *at* women *from* women, too. Often, it's more subtle than blatant. For instance, when it opened on Broadway, the musical comedy "Hairspray" got rave reviews. But this is what journalist Robin Pogrebin wrote in an August 21, 2002 *New York Times* article about the lead actress,

> *"Conventional wisdom holds that heavyset women shouldn't wear white because it accentuates their weight . . . Marissa Jaret Winokur, five feet tall and a size 11/12, wore white to the opening-night party of 'Hairspray' on Broadway . . . Heavyset women are often presumed to hate their bodies, to have low self-esteem, to want to hide."*

The article went on to marvel at the fact that Winokur somehow felt good about herself even wearing white short skirts and tight tops. *Why is this so unusual?* Because our culture doesn't allow it to be the norm.

Internet: The newest media

The Internet, a relatively new method of disseminating information, offers more of the "thin-is-in, antifat" messages. All you need is access to a computer and minimal skills to search for strategies to achieve that less-is-more look, and to find the "sales pitch" to make it seem appropriate. In fact, many websites that appear to advocate women's health give mixed messages to their readers. When I logged onto the "Diet and Fitness: safety and health" section of *iVillage.com* recently, a flashing banner ad at the top of the page showed a female's toned abdomen and the message, "If you want to cut the fat, cut the hype." That was followed by another banner that said, "Try the proven diet and fitness program from the editors of SHAPE magazine." So, even websites that seemingly promote women's psychological and physical well-being can actually impart a confusing message.

Boys and Men Aren't Immune

Even though the male "ideal" body varies from the extremes of physically huge, sometimes clinically obese, football players to lean marathon runners, more and more men are joining the dissatisfied-with-their-bodies group. According to the Alliance for Eating Disorder Awareness *(www.eatingdisorderinfo.org)*:

- One out of five men would trade three to five years of their lives to achieve their goal body weight!
- 40% of male football players surveyed in a Cornell University study engaged in some form of disordered eating.
- Of the people struggling with binge eating disorder, 40% are men.

Are You Sowing the Seeds of an Eating Disorder?

The physical changes you go through when you're a teenager are major ones. Growing into an adult body can be exciting, but it can also be frustrating, since you're never quite sure what the end result will be! This process can be further complicated if you don't have accurate information about predictable physical changes during adolescence. Did you know, for example, that young girls increase their percentage of body fat while guys decrease theirs?

So, having difficulty accepting your physical self, having problems accepting a discrepancy between your ideal body-image and the real one, and being misinformed about the physical changes during the teen years are some of the factors that can put you at risk for developing an eating disorder.

Be wary if you:

- buy into the "thin is in" mentality and attempt to achieve that image at all costs,

- look in the mirror and don't like what you see,

- negate compliments about your looks and make it seem like you're not worthy of them,

- don't often give yourself credit for the things you're good at;

- question how useful or valuable your ideas and opinions could be to someone else or to a group;

- feel misunderstood or ignored;

- fall into the habit of thinking and believing that you're never good enough or smart enough; and even if you're smart enough, that's not good enough!

I've always been embarrassed at being able to come in first at so many things I do in school. I feel like I should give others a chance to be first. I feel like a fraud a lot of the time because I'm not that much smarter or better than most of the other kids. I can't remember ever feeling 100% happy with myself or proud of myself.

– Sharyn H., age 17

On the other hand, you're less likely to be at risk if you:

- are usually realistic about your physical appearance and accept how you look without feeling disappointed in yourself,

- try to achieve a look that feels right for you even if it's not the "in" look,

- can accept compliments about your looks,

- usually feel comfortable in your own skin and can handle the natural changes in your body during a menstrual cycle and not "catastrophize" about a bit of bloat or added weight.

"When I Look in the Mirror" — A First Gaze Inward

Now do the following exercise, "When I Look in the Mirror." Complete each half-sentence. Write down the first things that pop into your head. Be honest, don't self-censor, and don't skip anything. Keep writing until all of your thoughts are in print on that piece of paper.

It can be both hard and scary to think about yourself in this way. But it's better to be scared than to keep your feelings so bottled up and hidden that you don't know what makes you tick. If you tap into and articulate what bothers you, odds are good that you will be able to make productive changes. "When I Look in the Mirror" can help you start the process.

Save this and any other written exercise you complete as you work your way through this book. Your responses will help you uncover the repetitive themes in your thinking and pinpoint areas you may need professional help to cope with, challenge, and/or change.

When I Look in the Mirror

1. When I look in the mirror, _____

_____

2. Today I looked in the mirror and _____

_____

3. I like myself best when _____

_____

4. The first thing I do when I get up in the morning is _____

_____

5. The first thing I think when I get up in the morning is _____

_____

6. I feel glad to be me when _____

_____

7. If my mirror could talk, it would say _____

_____

8. My perfect reflection would be _____

_____

9. The last time I liked what I saw in the mirror, _____

_____

10. My body is _____

_____

Did you respond with a lot of negatives, as in the following answers of people who were in treatment for anorexia and bulimia?

- "My body is gross and keeps me from being my best."
- "If my mirror could talk, it would say, 'You're hopeless.'"
- "I like myself best when I'm under 90 pounds."
- "The last time I liked what I saw in the mirror was never."

- "The first thing I do when I get up in the morning is weigh myself."
- "The first thing I think when I get up in the morning is, 'Who will I have to fool today?'"

If your answers have a *"downer" tone*, if they indicate you're really harping on weight, if your body-image is obviously distorted (for example, you *really* see yourself as fat when you're 5'8" and weigh 110 pounds), these are clues that you've taken the first steps toward developing an eating disorder.

"The Self-Esteem Test" is a final self-check, a quick way to summarize what has been discussed up to now and another way to pinpoint areas of possible concern for you.

The Self-Esteem Test

Choose the statement that best describes you. Most of the time, do you:

a. Accept compliments?   b. Negate them?

a. Consider the total picture of who you are and what you've accomplished?   b. Look for the blemishes (errors) in that total picture and dwell on them?

a. Like things about your physical self?   b. Look for and point out your physical shortcomings?

a. Reach a goal and savor it?   b. Reach a goal and think you could have done better or should have done more?

a. Like your friends and seek them out?   b. Tolerate your friends or try to avoid them?

a. Prefer the company of others?   b. Prefer solitude and isolation?

If you chose all the "a" answers, chances are you have high self-esteem and your self-image is in fine shape. If you chose all the "b" answers, you need to work on developing self-esteem, and you may be at risk for developing an eating disorder. If you chose some of each, ask yourself why you chose the "b" item rather than the "a" item!

Now What?

It's impossible to like or love yourself all the time. But if you rarely or never do, or if you really don't see how anyone else could feel positive emotions about you, you're at risk. Also, if you wall off your feelings for other people or become fearful of admitting you have feelings, you're in the process of building a protective cocoon around yourself and an eating disorder could be providing the thread with which you're weaving it.

There's an alternative, though. If you choose to read on, you'll learn to unravel that cocoon. You'll develop a self-image that is uniquely yours, instead of one that feels "imposed" on you by outside influences. You'll have the courage to challenge the negative self-talk and perceptions that result in a negative body-image, and discover (or rediscover) elements of your personality that will enhance your self-esteem.

And, finally, you'll discover (or rediscover) that true self-esteem does not depend on your outer appearance, but on knowing and accepting who you are, both inside and out. This entails taking a realistic look at all aspects of your mental, emotional, behavioral, and spiritual life with love and respect, without judgment, and making beneficial changes one step at a time.

Are you ready?

Ten Things to Remember about Self-Image, Body-Image, and Self-Esteem

1. The three interlinked elements of self-perception are: *self-image* (your sense of identity), *body-image* (how comfortable you are in your own skin), and *self-esteem* (the feelings you have about yourself).

2. Self-image is affected by a variety of influences and pressures you experience in your life, some of which are self-imposed, while others come from external sources.

3. Body-image, which develops over time and changes as you move through adolescence, is influenced by the three Ps: Parents, Peers, Press (the media).

4. In our culture, self-esteem is closely tied to body-image.

5. The "ideal" female form promoted by that culture is impossible for most of us to achieve. Most fashion models are thinner than 98% of American women.

6. People in thin bodies aren't always the healthiest, don't live the longest, and aren't necessarily happier or more loved than people whose bodies are heavier.

7. Your self-esteem drops when you lose sight of your positive qualities.

8. Eating disorders are more likely to occur when you're unhappy with your body-image and your self-image and self-esteem are at low points.

9. People who develop eating disorders tend to focus on negatives and ignore or discount the positives about themselves.

10. Boys and men also struggle with body-image issues and many of them develop eating disorders.

chapter three

When Habits Become Obsessions, Compulsions, or Addictions

"I know it's weird, but I knock on wood every time I talk about something good that's happened. I'm not always aware I'm doing it until a friend says, 'Why did you just do that?'"

– Mary Z., age 15

Habits are behaviors that we do over and over again, in the same ways, often under similar circumstances. Just about anything a person does can turn into a habit. Sometimes we don't know where or when the habits started and sometimes we make conscious choices to do things that later become our habits. Sometimes we're aware of our habits and even depend on them to help us get through each day; at other times, we hardly notice them.

Why do we develop habits? The truth is that without them our lives might become slightly chaotic. Habits impose order and structure and make it easy to do certain tasks. They also have the potential to enhance self-esteem by making us feel calm, secure, or at ease in various situations even if we aren't *consciously* aware of a connection between those habits and our feelings. Under certain circumstances, though, habits stop being helpful or comfortable and instead become physically and emotionally harmful, with negative ripple effects that are destructive to almost every aspect of our lives.

How Behaviors Become Habits

Take a moment to think about how you live your life each day. You'll soon realize that it's loaded with habits, from the way you roll out of bed or squeeze the toothpaste tube to the way you fluff your pillow and arrange the covers before going to sleep at night. Little habits that seem inconsequential when looked at individually are actually quite important as a group—they're part of what makes you a unique, social human being. Habits develop from once-in-a-while behaviors that have become useful to you for some reason. If they weren't useful, you wouldn't repeat the action often enough to make it a consistent part of your life! So, just about anything you might do has the potential to become a habit if the conditions are right.

What are those conditions? It depends. Habits develop in a context, which means that someone or something such as a feeling, a situation, a time of day, a person, or a place triggers them. You then react to the trigger with a behavior. For example,

- A baby is hungry, scared, or lonely. The baby reacts to those feelings by sucking its thumb. That thumb-sucking behavior becomes a habit and can persist long after the stress has passed, long after the child grows old enough to discuss things and seek other solutions.

- A teenager hangs out with a group of friends in high school who "high five" each time they pass one another in the halls. As an adult, this person gives the "high five" to colleagues at work—it has become his habit, a signal that recalls and represents good feelings and good relationships.

- As a child, you get praised for eating everything that you're served at mealtimes. You develop the habit of cleaning your plate even when you're not hungry, because the memory of the praise feels better than the discomfort of an overfull stomach. You then teach this same behavior to your children.

Habits, then, develop in response to a variety of situations. They also create results; what that result is—the impact—is also highly variable.

The Impact of Habits

The impacts of habits vary from positive to negative. On the positive side, they might take the edge off a tense situation, make you feel part of a crowd, get you noticed, or help you get a job done efficiently. They can also enhance your physical and emotional well-being.

> **On the negative side, habits can be enormously destructive in the long run, especially if they are behaviors over which you can lose control.**

One way to analyze a habit's impact is to visualize a *continuum*, a line that represents the range of possible ways any behavior (or series of behaviors) can affect your life.

The Habit-Impact Continuum

←――――――――――――――――――――――――――――――――――→

| Has positive impact | Rarely interferes, minor annoyance | Sometimes interferes or annoys | Often interferes or annoys | Has harmful, destructive impact |

The extremes of the continuum ("positive impact" and "harmful, destructive impact") are opposites. In between the two extremes is a broad and variable range of ways habits can affect you. The diagram shows a few of them.

Many habits have a positive impact or are virtually harmless, with just a minor annoyance rating. When was the last time that twirling your hair between your fingers or wearing your lucky outfit when you took an exam interfered with anything else you did? It's not likely such habits ever would. It's more likely that they'd be useful in some way, maybe as tension relievers. Some habits, especially those that are common courtesies (like holding the door open for the person behind you, waiting for everyone at the table to be served before starting to eat, or saying "thank you" when someone does something nice for you) usually result in similar courtesies coming your way. Some habits, which are harm*less* at certain times, can be harm*ful* at others.

> *"I jiggle my foot and leg a lot when I have to sit still at a desk. Today my foot slipped, I fell over backwards in the chair, knocked into the kid behind me, and got sent to the dean of students for disrupting the class. They thought I did it on purpose."*
>
> – Todd R., age 13

When Habits are Out of Control

Unfortunately, some habits that start out as once-in-a-while behaviors can turn into activities that completely dominate your thoughts to such an extreme that you become obsessed with them. Once obsessed, you feel a compulsion or urge to do them, in spite of knowing better.

This is basically what happens with the dieting patterns of anorexics or the bingeing and purging behaviors of bulimics. It also happens when anorexics have a binge-purge pattern that complicates their restricting. A habit can also become physically addictive if it involves excessive intake of alcohol, smoking, or recreational drug use.

In general, if

- a habit becomes so important in your life that you can't or won't function without using it as a crutch,

- you can't go for a reasonable amount of time without feeling an intense, inner pressure to perform that behavior,

- your mind is preoccupied with thoughts about the habit to an unnatural degree,

then the behavior has flipped into the harmful range and is no longer technically just a habit. It has become something much stronger and more central to your existence. This could take the form of an *obsession* (an idea or thought that persists even though you may not want it to), a *compulsion* (something you need to do over and over without really understanding why), or an *addiction* (a craving due to a physical and emotional dependency on substances like alcohol, nicotine, or drugs). Such behaviors are like habits gone crazy—out of control and very difficult to stop. They can throw your normal lifestyle off balance, damage your physical and mental health, and make life miserable for the friends and relatives around you.

> **Once the habit is transformed into something that controls you rather than something you can control, the impact is clearly destructive. At that stage, it can be very hard for you to regain control without professional counseling or medical intervention.**

Your Personal Habit Profile

Since habits are such personal, individualized behaviors, it's important to remember that how good or bad, safe or unsafe, useful or destructive a habit is depends in large part on the person and the situation involved. What's right for you might not be right for another person; what someone else can easily handle and control might turn into an obsession or compulsion for you.

Most of us have several types of habits: those we'd rather not have but don't make an effort to change because they don't interfere with anything; those we'd like to change but can't; and habits we *consciously* choose to maintain. The ideal situation is to be aware of your habits and keep them in balance so they won't fall toward the unsafe part of the habit-impact continuum.

A personal habit profile is a chart of your habits and the impacts they have on your life. No two people's personal habit profiles will look exactly alike. Also, as you grow and mature, your reactions to things like school or work, social life, family, and so on, change, so it's not unusual for any one person's habit profile to change from one period of time to another.

Creating your personal habit profile can:

- help you focus on your everyday behaviors and recognize things about yourself that might have slipped your notice;
- help you focus on how you think and talk about yourself;
- give you insight into what's going on in your life right now and why;
- help you see whether or not your habits are placing you on a self-destructive path.

To develop this personal habit profile, first sort out your existing habits. Pay attention to what you do during the course of a typical weekday (and/or night) and on a typical weekend day (and/or night). Jot down your observations. Put each habit in a spot on your habit-impact continuum. Then, you'll have created a personal habit profile, as in the following example:

Personal Habit Profile

Has positive impact	Rarely interferes, minor annoyance	Sometimes interferes or annoys	Often interferes or annoys	Has harmful, destructive impact

Here is what one person wrote up as her profile:

Positive impact	Minor annoyance	Sometimes annoys	Often annoys	Harmful impact
prompt, speak my mind, optimistic, am the first to offer to help someone in need	*chew too much gum, wear too much perfume*	*talk too loud, too much; put things off to last minute*	*interrupt conversations don't return phone calls, messy room, sloppy homework habits*	*smoke too much, shoplift, binge-eat at night, lie to parents*

Decoding Your Results

If you're satisfied with your personal habit profile, congratulations! But what happens if the majority of your habits fall into the less-desirable categories? Does that mean they are out of control? Does it mean you're on the road to developing an obsession, compulsion, or addiction? Should you worry?

The answer to each of these questions is, "It depends." As mentioned previously, habits must be evaluated in the context of where and when they occur as well as what triggers them. Also, a habit profile is changeable.

Keeping those factors in mind, ask yourself, "Are the habits affecting my life and everyone else's in a negative way?" "Have they been increasing in frequency and intensity?" "Do I manipulate people and circumstances so that I can engage in my habit?" If your answer to these questions is, "Yes," you need to carefully assess the seriousness of these behaviors. Also ask, "How long have I had these habits?" If you can't recall a time when they weren't part of your life, to change them will be a challenge, but not an insurmountable one.

> **The bottom line question is,**
> **"Who's in control: you or the habit?"**

When habits move in the direction of obsessions, compulsions, or addictions, it may feel like they have lives of their own. Their impact is negative. When any habit or group of habits is in control of you, you may look at life differently than you have in the past. You may be paying more attention to the thing you're obsessed with than to your friends, family, and school or work-related responsibilities. You may find that your interests become narrowly focused and eventually end up focused *only* on whatever it is that obsesses you. Your activities will be geared to satisfying that obsession, so what you actually do will appear compulsive, illogical, perhaps bizarre, and will be very resistant to change—either at someone else's suggestion or by your own attempts.

The Isolating Nature of Obsessions, Compulsions, or Addictions

People who *don't* have obsessions, compulsions, or addictions tend to have communication styles and habits that make it more comfortable and easier to relate to other people. A diagram of how they operate looks like a system of interlocking circles:

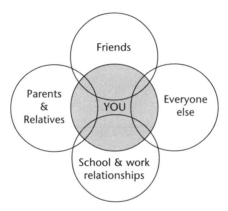

The circles overlap, which means that in real life the different people in the network interact with each other.

But the diagram looks different if your habits turn into obsessions, compulsions, or addictions. Instead of all overlapping circles, the one that represents you moves to a different position, as though you were in an outside orbit.

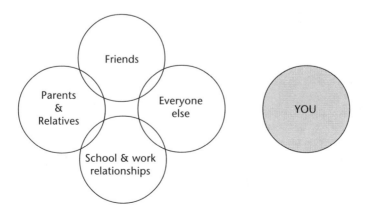

The person and the obsession, compulsion, or addiction become isolated, alone, and cut off from everything or everyone else that used to be a meaningful part of your life.

Habits Transformed into Eating Disorders

As we've seen, habits do not necessarily *lead* to obsessive behavior—*we all have habits*. But when habits morph into compulsive or obsessive behaviors, it is time to think seriously about what might be wrong. Often, when obsessions or compulsions have to do with food and eating, an eating disorder is likely to emerge.

When someone develops an eating disorder, a number of habits flip from the normal range to the destructive end of the continuum. Eating habits change drastically. In anorexia, food is not seen as life sustaining, but as an enemy to be avoided at all costs. At the same time, the anorexic becomes obsessed with the food that can't be consumed. With bulimia, cravings for certain foods develop into behaviors that mimic physical addictions. So, with anorexia and bulimia, normal eating habits are replaced by obsessive thoughts about food and compulsive dieting or bingeing and purging—acts that temporarily ease and satisfy the obsessions.

Invariably, relationships suffer. Communication with friends, family, and other people becomes limited and sometimes stops altogether. Isolation is preferred to socialization, and barriers, such as lying and secrecy, prevent healthy interaction with the people who make up your network of relationships.

Melinda P., a 16-year-old who had been anorexic and bulimic for two years before receiving professional therapy, discussed how the eating disorders affected her and called the description a "blanketing fog scenario." Here's part of it:

> The more I got into the dieting, and later on the more I binged
> and threw up, the less I cared about other things or people.
> Nothing mattered except that diet or the binge. I actually

forgot how to have fun with friends. I never talked much to my parents anyway, but when I was really into the anorexia and bulimia stuff I cut them out of my life completely.

I even built a barrier between the door of my room and my bed—where I spent most of my time—with my desk, on top of which I piled dozens of books about cooking, nutrition, even how to grow fruits and vegetables. It was my private fortress. The longer I did my thing, the more I felt like I was moving around in a fog—a blanketing fog that could shield me from everyone and everything I used to want to be around.

That fog feeling was really weird. I honestly believed no one would notice my habits had changed, because I thought no one would see through that fog. That lasted for months. But everyone noticed, and you know what's funny, no one could crack through that fog for a long time. It was like being in a womb. Or a tomb.

Lately, the Food Network on cable television has become popular, and many people with eating disorders make it a component of their own "private fortresses." Because the programming runs on a 24/7 schedule, it is always available to fuel the viewer's food obsessions and can be very triggering. It also can temporarily soothe the impact of emotional isolation and loneliness.

Obsessions, compulsions, or addictions are often terrible, but you don't have to be stuck with them for the rest of your life. The chapters that follow will show you how to confront these problems, take appropriate steps towards change, and succeed.

Ten Things to Know about Habits, Compulsions, Obsessions & Addictions

1. Habits are behaviors you do over and over in the same ways, under similar circumstances.

2. Habits develop as a response to something.

3. Habits have an impact.

4. The impact of habits varies from positive to negative, harmless to harmful.

5. Some habits can contribute to the development of an eating disorder.

6. An out-of-control habit is no longer harmless.

7. An obsession is an idea or thought that persists even though you may not want it to.

8. A compulsion is something you do over and over without understanding why.

9. An addiction is a craving due to a physical or emotional dependency that may need medical and psychological counseling to overcome.

10. When someone develops an eating disorder, a number of habits turn into obsessions or compulsions and become destructive.

chapter four

Straight Facts About Anorexia

When Not Eating
Becomes Your Obsession

"In many ways anorexia is stronger than grief, more abiding than love."

— Sandra H. Heater, *Am I Still Visible?*

norexia nervosa is a dangerous eating disorder that harms you both physically and mentally as you starve yourself in a quest for thinness. *Anorexia* means "loss of appetite," but that's misleading—when you are anorexic, you're almost always hungry. Through sheer willpower, stubbornness, and tenacity, you deny your hunger, learn to suppress it, and sometimes revel in its discomfort as proof of your strength and self-control.

"It is like a hand with sharp nails that's on top of my head holding me and hurting me. And in a way I like it because it cares for me even though it also hurts me. It holds my head really straight so I can only see in one direction."

— Gina S., age 20

Who Is Vulnerable?

We can say with certainty that anorexia nervosa affects many more females than males, regardless of their ages. The American Academy of Pediatrics Committee on Adolescence estimates that .5% of teenage girls and young women are anorexic. (*Pediatrics*, 2003;111:204-211) Other estimates, cited in various resources ranging from professional journals to online educational websites about eating disorders, suggest the number may be higher, between 1 and 4%. Approximately 0.2% of males are anorexic. But no one can say for sure that these statistics tell the whole story.

In addition,

- Approximately 10 to 20% of adolescent and young adult girls exhibit some, but not all, of the clinical symptoms of anorexia (i.e., occasional fasting, or bingeing and purging) but don't meet the criteria to be given a clinical diagnosis.

- Therapists, school counselors, physicians, and other health-care professionals report increasing numbers of elementary-school-age girls with anorexia, although accurate statistics for this group are not yet available.

- Many girls and boys express concern with being too fat as early as first grade, with 80% of girls in one study restricting their food intake by age 11 (Mellin) and 14% of first through fifth-grade boys in another study doing the same (Smolak and Levine).

Why are girls so vulnerable? Researchers Linda Smolak and Michael Levine think it's because most girls are smart enough to pick up cultural cues and will absorb the message that thinness is desirable *by the age of 13!* (We don't know *why* girls are so attuned to these cues; perhaps they "perceive" them differently than boys do, or perhaps "react" differently to them.) Although not all of these girls will become clinically diagnosed as anorexic, many become so focused on weight and shape that their moods and outlook on life are determined by the numbers on their scales. In either case, an obsession with slenderness has a definite negative impact on the quality of their lives.

Boys aren't immune to the lure of thinness. In August, 1997, *ELLE* magazine published an article titled "The Thin Man" which discussed the results of a survey of fifth- and sixth-grade boys, 43% of whom wanted to be thinner! Since role models for boys tend to be hefty sports figures, and since boys' toys, such as action and superhero dolls, are usually muscular, this statistic was surprising and unexpected. It points to a cultural shift which has made boys and men more vulnerable to the thinner-is-better message that has long influenced women and may now account for the increase in anorexic behavior and anorexia in high-school-age boys. Statistics don't yet reflect the hidden or incipient cases of anorexia, but certain populations of male athletes are vulnerable, notably the high-school boys who need to achieve low weights for certain sports (i.e., wrestling, boxing, track, swimming, crew) and must starve themselves to do so.

Recovery from anorexia is possible. However, the longer you have it, the harder it may be to recover. The good news is that some studies show recovery rates as high as 60 to 70% five years after treatment (Zerbe, p. 14). A study conducted by the Mayo Clinic concluded that most anorexics who receive treatment will recover (*www.medscape.com/viewarticle/450868*). The bad news is that fatalities occur in approximately 5% of the cases, and that number is likely to be higher the longer a person is ill (Zerbe, p. 250). Nonetheless, anorexia has one of the highest mortality rates of any mental illness.

Anorexia has taken its toll on many individuals who have been in the public eye. Singer Karen Carpenter was probably the first well-known celebrity to die as a result of complications caused by the binge-purge subtype of anorexia; world-ranked gymnast Christy Heinrich became anorexic after a judge said she was too fat to make the Olympic gymnastic team. At the time of that remark, she was 18 years old, 4'10', and weighed 93 pounds. When she died three years later, she weighed 47 pounds (Gayle, p. 3).

Websites that focus on famous people with eating disorders abound. Two of the current good ones are "Celebrities" (*www.caringonline.com/eatdis/people.html*) and "Theresa's World" (*www.geocities.com/angelqt94/eatingdisorder/celebs.html*). They include stories of celebrities past and present, such as Tracey Gold, Ally Sheedy, Sally Field, Janine Turner, and the late Princess Diana. Some recent additions to this list are Jamie-Lynn Sigler of "The Sopranos" and author of *Wise Girl*, pop singer Brandy, singer Victoria Beckham, a.k.a. Posh Spice, and the late Leila Pahlavi, daughter of the exiled Shah of Iran.

What Causes Anorexia?

There's never just one cause of anorexia. It is usually triggered by a *combination* of factors such as family dysfunction, romantic relationship problems, even something as seemingly harmless as someone else's casual remarks about your physical shape. It can be a reaction to growing up in an environment where you had to eat everything you were served and weren't allowed to express your preferences. It can develop from a lifelong habit of dieting and a belief system that equates thinness with success and happiness. It may be the ticket you're looking for that you think will make you part of the "in crowd" at your school. It may be your way of getting back at a parent, proving something, or getting yourself noticed.

> *When I was little, I'd get my revenge on my mother for going out without me. I learned how to make myself sick—I'd actually talk myself into getting a stomachache or a fever, and then she couldn't leave. Being anorexic is sort of the same thing—I look sick, I guess I am sick, and she has to pay attention.*
>
> *– Peri H., age 16*

The Role of Genetics and Heredity

There may also be a strong genetic component that acts as a risk factor for developing anorexia nervosa. An international group of researchers is currently trying to find out why eating disorders tend to run in families to such a degree that people whose mothers or sisters have been anorexic are 12 times more likely to develop anorexia than people with no family history of the disorder, and four times more likely to develop bulimia (for complete details of the research, go to *www.anbn.org*). Other research is focused on locating the actual genes that might increase someone's chance for developing the illness. An interested reader can find this study in the January, 2002 issue of the *American Journal of Human Genetics*. Studies of fraternal and identical twins have concluded that genetics plays a big role in the development of both anorexia and bulimia. But none of these studies is conclusive, many are ongoing, and the best we can say is that the data can help doctors and therapists come up with better ways treat and prevent these disorders.

The Controversy about Pro-Ana Websites

Anorexia is a powerful and seductive disorder. It is *so* seductive that a number of people have created websites that promote anorexia and an anorexic "life-style." Collectively referred to as " Pro-ana," these websites have been the subject of many debates since they surfaced and became popular online, circa 2000-2001.

In real life, an eating disorder isolates you from family and friends, but these sites create an artificial sense of community. Girls whose disorder demands secrecy, feel somehow safe "sharing" in an online life conducted in front of a computer monitor. Ironically, Pro-ana participants end up adding another layer of isolation to their existing ones in the name of "community" because while they *seem* to be interacting, in fact they're seated in front of their computers, most likely alone in their rooms, isolated from interaction with "real-life" family and friends.

The sites also play upon a psychological tendency we all have to some degree: *denial*. People who become severely anorexic and resist or refuse treatment usually deny that the illness is serious. These websites encourage such denial and make it that much harder for a family member or therapist to challenge the inaccurate belief.

Many Pro-ana sites were removed from Yahoo.com in 2001 and early 2002, but other search engines have allowed them to remain, based on the right to free speech. Some people feel there is value in such sites insofar as they provide a "lucid clarification of what it really feels like to be eating disordered" (Mimi Udovitch, "A Secret Society of the Starving," *New York Times Magazine*, September 8, 2002) and a place for some individuals to open up and be honest. Others are vehemently opposed to anything Pro-ana because it glamorizes something that is not at all glamorous. The validity of these websites is a matter of personal and/or professional opinion and isn't within the scope of this book to fully address. *The passion and anger generated by the websites, however, is indicative of how intensely someone can be ensnared by anorexia.*

Perhaps the following poem will illuminate the sense of desperation felt by someone with anorexia and clarify the allure a Pro-ana website has for someone who won't risk sharing such feelings anywhere else:

> *I can smell you, taste you, touch you*
> *I can swallow you, abuse you, refuse you.*
> *You can hurt me and nourish me or kill me*
> *I love you and hate you and despise you*
> *I want you but refuse you and miss you*
> *You make me ugly, big, and strong*
> *You make me obsessed, depressed, and regressed*
> *You're in my head, in my heart, and in my soul*
> *You invade my stomach*
> *Betray my power*
> *And put guilt in me*

You're my struggle, my grief, and my pain
Do you know you put my life in chains?

– Gina S., age 20

How Do You Know if You Have Anorexia?

The Eating Attitudes Test (EAT-26), developed by Drs. David Garner and Paul Garfinkel, has been used since 1979 as a quick way to determine if you have the symptoms of anorexia nervosa. It is so reliable that it was chosen to be used in the 1998 National Eating Disorders Screening Program, with a preventive purpose: early detection leads to appropriate treatment, which lowers a person's risk of severe health hazards or mortality from an eating disorder.

Take the test below. If you have access to a computer, you can also take the test online and have it scored immediately after submitting it. The website address is *www.river-centre.org/ED_Index.html*.

The Eating Attitudes Test (EAT-26)

1. Age
2. Sex
3. Height
4. Current Weight
5. Highest Weight (excluding pregnancy)
6. Lowest Adult Weight
7. Level of Education Completed

Choose one response for each statement.
Always – Usually – Often – Sometimes – Rarely – Never
1. Am terrified about being overweight.
2. Avoid eating when I am hungry.
3. Find myself preoccupied with food.
4. Have gone on eating binges where I feel that I may not be able to stop.
5. Cut my food into small pieces.

6. Aware of the calorie content of foods that I eat.

7. Particularly avoid food with a high carbohydrate content.

8. Feel that others would prefer if I ate more.

9. Vomit after I have eaten.

10. Feel extremely guilty after eating.

11. Am preoccupied with a desire to be thinner.

12. Think about burning up calories when I exercise.

13. Other people think that I am too thin.

14. Am preoccupied with the thought of having fat on my body.

15. Take longer than others to eat my meals.

16. Avoid foods with sugar in them.

17. Eat diet foods.

18. Feel that food controls my life.

19. Display self-control around food.

20. Feel that others pressure me to eat.

21. Give too much time and thought to food.

22. Feel uncomfortable after eating sweets.

23. Engage in dieting behavior.

24. Like my stomach to be empty.

25. Enjoy trying new rich foods.

26. Have the impulse to vomit after meals.

EAT © David M. Garner & Paul E. Garfinkel (1979), David M. Garner et al., (1982)

Scoring Instructions for the EAT-26

For all items except #25: Always=3, Usually=2, Often=1, Sometimes= 0, Rarely=0, Never=0.
For the item #25: Always=0, Usually=0, Often=0, Sometimes=1, Rarely=2, Never=3.

A score of more than 20 on the EAT-26 indicates excessive concerns that may indicate the presence of an eating disorder.

Be honest when you take this test. Although the score won't give you a definitive diagnosis of an eating disorder, you can use it to find out if you have a problem, how ingrained it is, or pinpoint troublesome eating-disordered thoughts and behaviors that may need a therapist's input to help you address and correct. If your score is 20 or above, you would be wise to seek professional help ASAP.

Understanding Anorexia

Anorexia is an obsession about *not* gaining weight, and as you get more frightened of eating, your whole routine begins to change. Ultimately, your personality and sense of identity become enmeshed with the anorexia, and all your efforts are geared to maintaining it.

You might weigh yourself several times a day and feel joy (if weight has been lost) or despair (if the scale shows a gain). Because of this preoccupation, you're likely to constantly look at yourself in mirrors to check the contours of your body, paying particular attention to the size of your hips, thighs, and stomach (and breasts if you're a girl). Ironically, if you've lost a large proportion of your total body weight (20 to 25%) you may still think you see an obese, bloated person in the mirror.

> **This is because such extreme weight loss causes chemical changes in your brain that alter your perception and make you see fat where there is none.**

To hide the imagined fat, you may start wearing hugely oversized (not just fashionably large) clothes. On the other hand, you may be so proud of your concave stomach and protruding shoulder blades, collarbone, ribs, and hipbones, you may elect to wear skin tight, low-ride pants and mini tops to flaunt your thinness.

When my weight hovers around 90 pounds (I'm 5'5") I see how absolutely skinny I am and how awful I look. But when it dips down to 88 or less, all I see is a gross, fat person and I want to hide.

– Missy P., age 16

Eating Habits

If you have anorexia, you hate fat (maybe even fear it) and deny yourself the right to eat the way most people do. You may ban red meats and processed meats (such as bologna and hot dogs) from your diet altogether and restrict yourself to eating small amounts of white meat, poultry, and non-fatty fish. You cut out foods such as mayonnaise, peanut butter, hard cheeses, butter and margarine, and avoid sweets and desserts, processed breads and sugary cereals. If confronted, you justify your food choices by saying you know a lot about nutrition and you're just "eating healthy" by cutting down on fats and cholesterol in your diet. You probably allow yourself certain "safe" foods such as low-calorie vegetables, crunchy fruits such as apples, salads with vinegar (balsamic is a favorite) or no-oil salad dressings, plain popcorn, unsalted rice cakes, low-fat cottage cheese, and nonfat yogurt, but only in limited amounts.

Many of you say that you are vegetarian; so many, in fact, that a study published in 2001 found adolescent vegetarians as a group are more likely than their non-vegetarian peers to be weight and body conscious, to have tried unhealthy weight-control techniques such as diet pills, laxatives, and vomiting, to have contemplated or attempted suicide, and to have been diagnosed as eating disordered by a doctor *(Adolescent Health* 2001;29:406-416).

To be anorexic doesn't mean you're not interested in food, though. Quite the contrary—you're involved in (and maybe obsessed with) every aspect of food: what to purchase, how to prepare it, and who should eat it, as long as the "who" is *not* yourself.

When I was at my very worst—I think I got down to 82 pounds and I'm 5'7"—I bought my mom two cookbooks and an encyclopedia of Japanese cooking. I also charged a $250 meat order on my mom's credit card from a mail-order beef company's Christmas catalogue. For two months I prepared every single dinner at home and made all the brown-bag lunches for my little brother and sister. I wouldn't let them

*near the refrigerator. I felt like the kitchen was all mine. I ate
no more than 250 calories a day and kept a notebook about
what I ate. I must have really wanted to torture myself. When
we were in family therapy one evening, my mom said I was
like a drug pusher, only I was pushing food.*

— Antoinette L., age 17

Sometimes you lose your self-control and start to binge, flipping
into a bulimic pattern that makes you feel guilty and scared. So you
purge, the way a bulimic would, and then go back to your anorexic
habits. This is so common that *DSM-IV-TR* (American Psychiatric
Association), the medical reference book used by health care professionals to help them diagnose mental health problems, has distin-
guished between a "restricting" type of anorexia in which the person basically doesn't eat, and a "binge-eating/purging" type in which
the person regularly binges and purges and then goes into an anorexic
phase, only to binge and purge again (p. 589). This seesaw routine
can go on indefinitely.

Private Rituals

You might develop private rituals to divert your attention from
the physical discomfort of hunger and block out the eating disordered thoughts bombarding your brain. Without the rituals you
might have trouble doing even the most ordinary things. For example, you may need to touch a certain piece of furniture before
walking out the door, make yourself do one hundred sit-ups for each
bite of food you allow yourself to eat, or break off half of every pret-
zel or cracker and throw it on the floor before you let yourself eat
the other half. You may only swallow food after you've chewed each
mouthful a set number of times, not allow an eating utensil to touch
your lips, cut your food into tiny pieces, not wash the dishes you've
used until the end of the day so you can count them, and so on.
Rituals are as unique as the person who creates and performs them.

You tend to get very strict about these rituals and don't like anyone to interfere when you're performing them. You also lose your sense of humor as you become more and more rigid, doing the same things in the same ways. In some people, this rigidity is reflected in handwriting that becomes uncharacteristically small and neat or in drawings that are extremely detailed. Some behaviors may develop that seem logical to the person with the eating disorder, but are illogical to anyone else:

> *I cannot go to sleep at night unless I first go downstairs to my freezer and put my hands in the ice cube container. I count to 90 or until my hands begin to feel numb and I shiver. That way I think I am burning more calories than I normally would and it makes me believe I will lose weight when I sleep. When I first became anorexic, I would put ice cubes on my body when I was lying in the empty bathtub, hoping it would melt the fat wherever I put the ice. But that was too hard to do in secret, so I switched to this bedtime ritual. Do other anorexics do this?*
>
> – Troya S., age 17

Do other anorexics do this? The answer is "yes," other anorexics do similarly odd things, many of which are factually erroneous and even potentially dangerous. Keeping your mind off your hunger and onto the commitment to lose weight (when you don't need to and when your body is sending you signals *not* to), can take a lot of time and energy.

> *I'm so regimented and I need such control that it's exhausting. I feel like I don't give my body enough energy, so everything is taxing, everything is a frigging ordeal. I can keep my life very small and very controlled but I hate it. I'm so tired.*
>
> – Sara P., age 19

Social Withdrawal and Isolation

As the anorexia progresses, you lose tolerance for things and people you used to like. You become very self-centered and choose to isolate yourself as much as possible. When you do reach out and try to spend time with other people, you often alienate them. If you ask for advice, you're likely to reject it immediately; you want your opinions to be accepted without question or you get insulted and defensive. Since you cannot accurately see how your body looks, you assume that anyone who challenges your vision is wrong. Often, you can't see the other person's point of view and may not even want to.

You may stop taking your phone calls, refuse to go out with friends, and eventually you may refuse to go out at all.

> I can't make phone calls anymore because I am so afraid my friends will find me boring or stupid or won't see things the way I do. I know people talk about me behind my back. I hear them sometimes in the hall near my locker and anytime I walk past the cafeteria. I can't go in. I won't go in there. And I don't answer my phone if it rings, which isn't often these days. I have caller ID and voice mail, and even if a friend calls, I think it's because of pity. I'm so sad. This isn't me, but it is me.
>
> – Andrea T., age 14

At this stage of anorexia, it's not unusual to skip school or work, stay in sweats or pajamas all day, and to stop the basic grooming that you'd otherwise do without a second thought—like showering, combing your hair, and brushing your teeth. Some people are literally afraid to look at themselves when they are naked, and others can't touch themselves when showering or bathing because they become fearful of the flesh on their bodies. Others become obsessive about a specific area of the body and will pinch themselves or measure, over and over again, the circumference of a wrist or upper arm to gauge the amount of imagined fat that has been gained or lost.

Physical Complications

As you lose more and more weight (especially if you reach that dangerous mark of 20 to 25% of your acceptable, "normal" weight) your body undergoes some dramatic physical changes. Your face and body take on an emaciated appearance. Your eyes may seem vacant and hollow, your bones protrude, and your stomach and chest seem to cave in. Your hair falls out and you may develop fine, downy hair (lanugo) on other parts of your body. Your skin changes in color and texture—it gets dry and rough, sometimes purplish or darker than normal. Sometimes your skin becomes yellow-tinged due to a condition called "hypercarotenemia" which is present in more than 80% of anorexics. The cause is not known and seems to be unique to the form of malnutrition that results from anorexia. Your fingernails take on a bluish tinge, which may extend to your wrist bones. It may also occur from your toes to above your kneecaps. Sometimes your fingernails develop ridges.

Sleep Problems

Sleeping can become a problem, in part because it can be painful to lie down if you've lost too much weight and there isn't enough fat left on your body to cushion your bones. You might not be able to sleep because you're so hungry that your mind is flooded with thoughts and images of food and eating (or not eating). You may push yourself to stay up past the point of exhaustion, fighting off sleep, because you believe that the *struggle* to stay awake burns extra calories. (This is not true, by the way, but it's another example of the erroneous ideas that make anorexia so hard to dispute.) You may be physically cold most of the time and discover that moving around a lot helps warm you, so you become compulsive about exercising. The exercise also gives you an excuse to allow yourself to eat, because you will burn off the calories in your workout.

Muscle and Bone Changes

If you don't have enough fat on your body, your muscles will be used for food and fuel, so your muscle tone decreases. Since the heart is really a large muscle, anorexia puts it in great physical danger; both its capacity to work efficiently and blood pressure in response to exercise will be reduced. When the heart is tested with an electrocardiogram, abnormalities, such as irregular beat, are often discovered. Death in anorexic patients is often due to cardiac complications; in most cases, death is sudden.

You may experience pain in your muscles, joints, and bones. Such pain can mean that you have developed *osteoporosis* (a disease that thins your bones and makes them fragile and thus easy to break) as a result of the self-starvation. You may even have stress fractures in those bones. Or you may have *osteopenia*, a less severe loss of bone mineral density (BMD) but one which signals hormonal and nutritional deficiencies serious enough to require medical attention.

Several studies have confirmed that bone loss is a serious complication of anorexia and is difficult to reverse.

Ninety-two percent of the sample of anorexic women in their mid-20s studied at the Massachusetts General Hospital had osteopenia in either the spine or hip areas (*Annals of Internal Medicine,* November 21, 2000). Of those, more than 50% had osteopenia at the spine and almost 25% had osteoporosis there; 47% had osteopenia at the hip and 16% had osteoporosis there. The women who weighed the least showed the most serious loss of bone. Estrogen deficiency (as indicated by loss of menstrual periods) was most highly linked with loss of bone density in the spinal region. Unfortunately, neither estrogen, calcium, nor Vitamin D supplements had any positive effect on bone density of the hip or spine in any of the research subjects! Another study done at the same hospital found that even when the nutritional status of anorexic girls improved in a year's time, the bone mineral density improved more slowly than in girls who had no history of anorexia (*Journal of Clinical Endocrinological Metababolism, Sept. 2002, 87–9:4177-85*).

Researchers in Denmark believe that anorexia may cause permanent skeletal damage that is later made worse by the normal bone loss that occurs with aging. This study found that compared with non-eating-disordered people, anorexic patients were approximately twice as likely to break a bone; the risk remained for up to 10 years post-diagnosis! (*International Journal of Eating Disorders, 2002, 32:301-308*). For a more thorough discussion of osteoporosis and bone density testing, an excellent resource is the Mayo Foundation for Education and Research, *www.mayoclinic.com.*

Another interesting Harvard study based on interviews with hundreds of ninth and tenth grade girls found that those girls had a higher chance of suffering bone fractures if they drank cola—five times greater than those who didn't drink any sodas! Although the reason for this is not 100% certain, it may be due to the fact that colas have phosphoric acid, that potentially affects how the body metabolizes calcium, which affects the development of bone mass. Or it may be due to the fact that girls who drink sodas drink less milk to begin with (*New York Times*, 6/20/00, F8) and therefore have less calcium with which to develop strong bones. Since many girls with anorexia drink enormous quantities of diet sodas, this study can point to one source of an anorexic female's bone density problems.

Hormones

If you're female and anorexic, your periods may stop (or not start at all if you hadn't menstruated before you developed anorexia). The good news is that various studies have shown that menstruation resumes in a large percentage of women who manage to return to ideal body weight. Many doctors will prescribe a choice of hormone replacements, such as birth control pills, to help get the menstrual cycle started. It's important to discuss this option with your physician and understand the physical changes that are likely to occur as you start the hormone replacement therapy. It's also important to remember that the pills alone *without appropriate nutrition* aren't sufficient to conquer the physical effects of anorexia.

Blood Sugar

You may also have problems with your blood sugar levels, which are most commonly on the low side in anorexics. You may feel listless, tired, exhausted, unfocused, "zoned," or disoriented. You may have cold sweats or heart palpitations, feel panic, or faint. If your blood sugar levels get too low, you are at risk for sudden death. It is very important to have a minimum of 300 to 400 calories of glycogen stored in your liver, in case you have not eaten appropriately (this is why marathon runners will load up on carbohydrates before a race, for example). Most anorexics don't have adequate stores of glycogen.

Other Physical Issues

You may have constipation problems. Your gastric emptying rate (the time it takes for food to be digested, pass through your system, and be excreted) is much slower than it would be if you were eating sufficient amounts of food in a more regular pattern. In some cases, it can take from four to eight days for a meal to be eliminated after an anorexic begins to eat again.

> **Because of the slowness, you will have an exaggerated sense of feeling full and satisfied after eating—you'll think you've had enough, but your body would really like you to eat more.**

You may have abdominal pain, because your stomach is smaller than it would be if you ate normally and it can't seem to accept what you are eating. Sometimes, in addition to ordinary constipation, which can usually be corrected by adding high fiber foods to your diet and giving your body time to adjust, a more severe situation can develop. This is called "fecal impaction," in which the digested material in the bowel cannot be excreted but is literally stuck in place. It has to be removed by a healthcare provider such as a nurse or physician.

If you are bingeing or purging alternately with the starvation pattern, you may have severe heartburn because of vomiting or because stomach acid seems to make its way up into your throat (acid reflux), both of which irritate the lining of the esophagus and the pharynx. If you try to drink milk of any kind or eat anything with milk protein, you may also experience heartburn. Many anorexics have severe edema (swelling), often most noticeable in the fingers and legs, but sometimes seen as facial puffiness, which is caused by a loss of sodium chloride (salt). This puffiness is distinct from the facial puffiness of bulimia caused by swelling of the parotid glands. Edema can also occur if you use diuretics.

Interpersonal Relationships

Not only does anorexia affect your body and your personality, it also changes the way other people relate and react to you. When you're severely emaciated, people who haven't seen you for a while may actually pull away when you meet because they're afraid of what they're observing and unsure of how to react. People who are in touch with you on a regular basis often vacillate between being overly kind and sweet, treating you as if you were feeble and fragile, and trying a "get tough" tactic with you to convince you to give up your anorexia, by threatening, ranting, and fighting with you.

Things can go from bad to worse at home, especially if you have brothers or sisters. They may be jealous of the attention you're getting because you're anorexic. They may try to drive a wedge between you and your parents in order to get some of that attention for themselves. If they're little, they may try to mimic what you do at mealtimes. If they're older, they may taunt you. Instead of having siblings to support you, you may end up with siblings who try to sabotage you.

Your parents can even get into battles with each other. They may not agree on how to handle you. One parent may feel left out if you seem to be closer to the other. Their own relationship may suffer and they may try to make you feel guilty and responsible for their problems. Sometimes it may seem they want you to do one thing and will tell you so, then change their minds in the middle of a conversation and tell you something contradictory. This is called a *mixed message* or a *double bind*. They may do this so often that you feel they are *consistently inconsistent* and you may become frustrated and angry, which may make it even more difficult to give up your eating disorder.

> *We had Senior Skip Day on Monday, and my friends and I were planning to go to Six Flags. My parents spent one whole hour haranguing me about how I couldn't go, it wasn't safe, it'd be dangerous for me and I'd have a problem, and then they turned it around to saying, "You have to make decisions for yourself and not because we tell you to," and so I felt like no matter how I chose, I wouldn't please them. But I went anyway, and I couldn't make myself eat that day, I was so nervous.*
>
> – Liz M., age 18

Sometimes you may use the anorexia to get your parents to pay close attention to you, even though your actions and reactions suggest the opposite. Unfortunately, if you are anorexic you may believe that you need to be sick in order to be cared for and cared about, or to be heard and taken seriously.

Before the eating disorder got so strong, I wanted to look good; now I want to look sick, maybe because I want to hurt some people. For sure it has to do with my parents. But I also want them to take control, to care for me . . . . Maybe I don't have enough self-confidence to think people will care for me if I don't have an eating disorder.

– Jenny H., age 17

Another common theme is that without the anorexia you will "disappear," almost as if you will become invisible to your family and friends.

> **Ironically, it is the anorexia that cloaks you with a kind of invisibility: the "essence" of your personality becomes hidden under the rules and rituals of the disorder.**

In the later stages of anorexia, your voice can literally become very small, like a whisper. The words you speak are often tentative, your sentences terse, with confusion and ambivalence peppering the things you say.

Since sex is a form of communication, and since anorexia alters how you communicate all aspects of your "self," physically intimate experiences are often transformed from occasionally awkward to frightening. Many anorexics report completely losing their sexual feelings and sex drive. This may be a result of hormonal deficiencies but also may be due to a psychological walling-off of emotions, a profound lack of trust in interpersonal relationships, a fear of being naked, a literal fear of being touched and of touching someone else. Sexual dysfunction is a complicated and serious side-effect of this disorder.

Mixed Messages and Mistaken Notion of "Control"

Do you remember the previous discussion of mixed messages and double binds? It can also be *you* giving your family and friends the mixed messages: you want to be heard and taken seriously, but the behaviors you are engaged in make that very difficult. You want people to pay attention to you, yet when they do so, you argue or withdraw from their scrutiny.

> **With anorexia, you lose the ability to see yourself as others see you.**

You may have trouble understanding or agreeing with their concerns for your health and well being. You think you're on your way to achieving a very important goal and assume everyone who challenges you is jealous. You're able to ignore the reactions and rejection of people who have been part of your life, because the anorexia makes you believe you're strong and superior, in spite of the fact that others see and say that it's making you ill. However physically ill or weak you feel when you're starving yourself this way, however lonely and isolated you are, such things are secondary to the sense of power you believe you have over yourself and your hunger. And because they're secondary, you don't try to fix them.

That sense of control and power will feed you (in the absence of actual food), and it will give you the impetus to continue your disordered patterns. Ironically, though, if you're anorexic, it's the anorexia that has the real control over you.

You're trapped. The anorexic voice in your head is like that of a sleazy friend who is trying to make you believe in things you know are wrong, and make you do things that would normally go against your better judgment. The anorexia makes you think that it is your ally and everyone else is the enemy—a perspective that's very tough to challenge and change. That's why fighting anorexia nervosa can be so hard—it feels like you're fighting yourself.

It Takes Time and Effort to Heal

It takes strength and stubbornness to be anorexic, but that same power and persistence can be used to free yourself of the disorder. You have to believe in the process of recovery, give yourself permission to heal, and take the time you need to do it.

> *Every day the food obsession is becoming less and less important to me. I have to admit that some days are pretty bad, but those days are occurring less frequently. I'm really happy with my progress and I WILL NOT start going backwards.*
>
> – Ellen S., age 15

Is it worth the effort? Definitely.

Ten Things to Remember about Anorexia

1. Anorexia is a self-starvation disorder that primarily affects females, although the number of males with anorexia is increasing.

2. Anorexia is triggered by a combination of factors: physical, emotional, social, familial, genetic.

3. As your personality and sense of identity become tied to being anorexic, your daily routine changes to maintain the disorder, you lose tolerance for people and things you used to like, and isolate yourself.

4. As anorexia progresses and your eating becomes restrictive, ritualized, and obsessive, your body will undergo dramatic physical changes.

5. Extreme weight loss causes chemical changes in your brain that alter your perception and makes you see fat where there is none.

6. Anorexia changes the way other people relate and react to you.

7. Some individuals with anorexia also binge and/or purge. An accurate diagnosis is therefore important in order to receive appropriate treatment.

8. A typical but inaccurate belief of many anorexics is that you need to be sick to be heard and taken seriously, because without the anorexia you will "disappear" and become invisible to family and friends.

9. Anorexia makes it almost impossible for you to see yourself as others see you.

10. It takes strength and stubbornness to be anorexic, and that same power and persistence can be used to free yourself of the disorder.

chapter five

Straight Facts About Bulimia

When Bingeing and Purging Becomes Your Obsession

"Maybe I have to start eating foods that I think are "bad" bit by bit so I'm not afraid of them. I guess it won't happen all at once but I feel so stupid for not being able to do it all at once! I want to stop throwing up totally. Or at least get through one whole day."

– Allie G., age 15

Bulimia is another eating disorder that can be harmful to your physical and mental health; like anorexia, it can result in death. Also, like anorexia, it is fueled by a dual obsession with both thinness and food. In fact, these two eating disorders have been called "Cinderella's stepsisters" and are often referred to as flip sides of the same coin. Unlike anorexia, which prompts you to starve yourself, bulimia (which literally means "ox hunger") is most often a binge-purge pattern in which you feel an overwhelming urge to binge (eat a large amount of food in a short period of time) and then an equally overwhelming urge to purge (eliminate) from your body whatever foods and liquids were consumed during the binge.

Methods of purging vary. Some bulimics make themselves vomit, while others abuse laxatives, emetics (medications that make you vomit), diuretics (chemicals that rid your body of fluids), enemas, diet pills, or a combination of these. *Any method a bulimic person uses to purge is potentially dangerous, because it can have serious physical and emotional consequences.*

Some individuals with bulimia don't purge, but instead alternate between bingeing and barely eating at all. This is called *non-purging bulimia.* When you struggle with this form of the disorder, along with the binges, you are likely to be preoccupied with your body's shape and weight, exercise to extremes, or diet and/or fast. You might even chew your food and then spit it out without swallowing in order to avoid gaining weight. Because it is sometimes difficult to distinguish variants of bulimia from variants of anorexia (such as "anorexia nervosa, binge-purge subtype"), any diagnosis should be made by a competent health-care professional so that appropriate treatment can be obtained.

Bulimic "hunger" is most often emotionally driven. A bulimic binge may initially give you a rush, or provide you with an emotional outlet—a "letting go" of pressures and restrictions. A purge provides a similar release, but both binge and purge components are physically painful and often frightening. When you're in the midst of a binge, you feel as if you have little or no control over your eating behavior. Paradoxically, while a purge might seem like a way of regaining that control, you seem to have no choice about whether or not to do it. So, in actuality, purging can *also* make you feel "out of control."

Although bulimia is more prevalent than anorexia, it is more difficult to detect since many bulimics are normal weight, or at least not obviously underweight. The physical cues such as swollen parotid glands below the jawline, knuckles that are scarred as a byproduct of self-induced vomiting, broken blood vessels under your eyes from purging, are often ignored or misattributed. So, it's not uncommon for bulimics to deny that they are ill, and, *in the beginning,* it's relatively easy to hide the disorder.

Once established, however, the binge-purge pattern is difficult to hide or change *even if you want to.* It can mimic an addiction: the more you do it, the more you want and need to do it. So, for some people, it becomes an actual addiction.

Who Gets It and Why?

Theoretically, anyone can get bulimia; fortunately, not everyone does. Bulimia tends to affect individuals who are easily influenced by media and already hypersensitive about weight and body- image issues. Many have struggled with erratic eating patterns, or have family, friends, teachers or coaches who are similarly focused. Often, bulimia surfaces after someone has previously battled anorexia.

The fantasy that bulimia is a relatively easy and safe way to have your proverbial "cake" and then be able to "eat it too" without suffering unintended weight gain or health consequences, is very seductive. Unfortunately, it doesn't accomplish either goal.

> **Bulimia is neither easy nor safe. Instead, it can destroy your mental, emotional, spiritual, and physical health, and manipulate your daily life, relationships, and hopes for the future.**

Like anorexia, bulimia affects more females than males. It's estimated that between 1 and 5% of adolescent girls and young women in the United States struggle with this disorder (*Pediatrics*, 2003;111:204-211). But there *are* many male bulimics, and estimates suggest that men account for between 10 and 20% of bulimic patients.

The most typical age range for bulimia to begin in earnest is between 16 and 18, a point at which someone may actually be in the process of separating physically and emotionally from home and is apt to have more personal freedom—a driver's license, a job (hence, extra cash for binge foods), large blocks of time away from family (and, presumably, more privacy).

However, the disorder has been steadily creeping into the pre-teen age groups. Several factors predispose a preteen to becoming bulimic:

- Self-esteem issues (such as negative self-evaluation, shyness, perfectionism);

- Social problems (such as having few friends, being bullied);

- School-related problems (such as school avoidance and/or truancy, conduct problems);

- Physical development issues (such as early menstruation, obesity);

- Emotional problems (such as depression);

- Parents who struggled with depression;

- Family issues about eating (such as family dieting, tension at family meals, critical comments regarding eating);

- Parenting style issues (such as over-involvement, under-involvement, absence, or discord between parents);

- Parents who struggled with obesity and/or other eating disorders.

Bulimia, then, can sometimes be a learned behavior, one that is "modeled" by people you know who seem to use it as a response to stress or as a problem-solving technique. It can develop within the context of your family, as the above list shows. But often it's "learned" within a different kind of family—your peers. The fact that bulimia is rampant, especially in high school and college, is therefore understandable. When people are in close contact socially and emotionally, they can learn the rationale and techniques of bingeing and purging from one another. They become desensitized to the dangers of the pattern, perhaps even trivialize or "normalize" it within the context of school life. Away from home and parental scrutiny, many pick up the behavior without realizing the point at which it becomes an addictive habit. "It's no big deal," "It's weekend stuff," "It's part of the tension blow-off" are comments you might hear from individuals in denial about the gravity of the problem. But bulimia *is* a big deal, and it *should* be taken seriously.

Comorbidity: The Depression-Bulimia Link

Sometimes an eating disorder is just the tip of the iceberg, and some susceptible individuals struggle with two or more categories of emotional, physical, or behavioral problems. This is called "dual diagnosis" or "comorbidity."

One of the most common conditions that occurs with bulimia is depression, which affects between 50 and 65% of bulimic women (T. Pearlstein, "Eating disorders and comorbidity," *Archives of Women's Mental Health (2002) 4:67-78.*) People who suffer from depression have symptoms such as losing interest in things they used to love to do, feeling dejected or hopeless, experiencing changes in how their bodies function, feeling tired out of proportion to their physical activity, having school problems, and thinking about suicide. Bulimia often develops in response to or along with the depression.

More examples of comorbidity are shown in the following statistics: 71% of bulimic women have some kind of anxiety disorder and of those, 59% have social phobia. About one-third have a kind of seasonal affective disorder in which eating disorder symptoms increase in severity in the winter (Pearlstein, 2002). An interesting study has shown that bulimic symptoms seem to be relieved by simple light therapy (Mark Moran, "Light Therapy Lessens Bulimics' Binging and Purging," *WebMD Medical News*, April 6, 2001).

Genetics also seem to play a role in the depression-bulimia connection. Researchers already know that if you've had a close relative with depression, you're at greater risk for developing the same illness.

Additional Comorbid Situations: Risk-Taking Behaviors

It's not unusual for bulimic symptoms to also coexist with other risk-taking behaviors. Many people who develop bulimia also struggle with alcohol and/or drug abuse. Some have problems with impulse control and get in trouble for shoplifting and other forms of theft. Many bulimics are also "cutters" who self-mutilate at times. (This is also true of anorexics who have a binge-purge variety of the disorder.) *If any of these situations applies to you, it's important to own up to them so that all components of your particular set of challenges will be addressed in therapy.*

What Makes a Binge "Bulimic"?

How someone defines a binge is a very personal matter. One person might describe it in terms of the quantities of food eaten in a short time span. Another person might consider that eating certain *kinds* of foods constitutes a binge, regardless of the amount or time frame. Occasionally, a person will label eating just a tiny quantity of a "forbidden" food to be a binge, like one piece of candy, or a spoonful of ice cream. It all depends on the person's interpretation.

Note that overeating *in and of itself* does not lead to bulimia. Some binges are just splurges, mini self-indulgences that are fun and filled with the appreciation of food and the people with whom you share it. Some are opportunities to let off steam, reward yourself for an accomplishment, take a break in your routine, or give yourself a time-out from tedium. If you know why you're eating in this way, you don't follow the binge by a purge, or you don't find that occasional overeating or splurging interferes with how you live your life or think about your self-worth, your binge is *not* bulimic behavior.

Generally speaking, bulimic binges are terrifying, out-of-control experiences that become intense, dominant, negative forces in your life. They hurt physically, are increasingly habit-forming, and are often accompanied by feelings of self-loathing. They are typically followed by a purge of some sort.

A binge is something I do because I have to, not because I want to. A binge is like some medieval torturer subjecting me to things I wouldn't allow done to myself if I could help it.

– Arlie M., age 18

A binge? A binge is eating and not tasting. I feel like a trash compactor—shovel it in, smash it, throw it out. Over and over, the same thing. I waste a lot of time and energy on this and I wish I didn't have to.

– Lydia Z., age 17

Every aspect of the binge-purge cycle can make you feel guilty, depressed, and/or out of control. You can feel angry, spacey ("zoned out"), nervous, disgusted with yourself, panicky, lonely, and inadequate before, during, and after a binge and/or purge episode. These feelings are very difficult to shake off, and might even propel you into your next binge, in an endless cycle of self-abuse.

Are You Bulimic?
A Checklist of Bulimic Behavior and Self-Talk

Do any of the following statements apply to you?

- My life would be better than it is now if I were thin.
- I'd be more sociable and popular if I were thin.
- I like to eat but I refuse to gain weight.
- I hoard food in my room.
- I eat even if I'm not hungry.
- I rarely know when I'm hungry or when I'm full.
- I have used some or all of the following to control my weight: laxatives, diet pills, diuretics, enemas, fasting, vomiting, emetics.

- I spend a lot of money each week on foods that most people consider "unhealthy" or "junk."
- I would consider stealing food or money if I didn't have enough money to buy the binge foods.
- I binge on large amounts of food that I eat rapidly and may not even really taste.
- I binge in private.
- I eat until I'm too exhausted to continue or it hurts too much to continue.
- I'm uncomfortable eating in public; I have trouble doing so.
- I'm afraid that if I order what I want at a restaurant, people will think bad things about me.
- I control my weight by purging.
- I can make myself vomit.
- I don't think it's a problem if I make myself throw up once in a while; many of my friends do it.
- I deal with a lot of the tension in my life by bingeing and purging.
- I am impulsive.
- I often feel sad, down, depressed.
- Food dominates and maybe even controls my life.

This list is not meant to be exhaustive, but includes many typical thoughts and behaviors of bulimics and the situations in which they find themselves. If your sense is that, "This is me!" you might be in the process of developing or may already have developed bulimia. Use the list as a way to pinpoint areas of particular concern, and to help you describe your situation when and if you choose to get professional help.

The Evolution of a Bulimic Habit

Bulimia transforms the meaning and significance of eating into a self-destructive activity that makes it just about impossible to eat normally and unselfconsciously. Food becomes an antagonist rather than a source of pleasure and a way to socialize with others. Eating becomes disconnected from anything that would nourish you either physically or emotionally. How does this happen? Let's look at a typical case.

Let's say you're a person who takes the "thin-is-in" cultural bias very seriously. This creates two warring impulses: you want to be thin *and* you want to eat. Your eating habits might be a little extreme (like those of most teenagers); in other words, you overeat occasionally and then diet afterwards because you're afraid to gain weight. Maybe you even fast for a day or two or try some non-prescription diet pills from a local grocery or drugstore.

> **The problem with this approach is that your metabolism slows down to conserve energy and prepare for the "famine" it senses is forthcoming when you diet or fast.**

So, if you go off the diet and return to your old eating habits without making any adjustments (like moderately increasing your exercise level), you're likely to gain weight *faster* because your metabolism has become accustomed to burning calories more slowly. If you try to diet again, the same situation will probably happen again when you stop. You might now weigh more than when you started: you've become a "yo-yo dieter," which means your weight goes up a bit after each loss of weight, hence the image of a yo-yo on a string.

But you don't like the weight gain! You find out about purging and decide to try it. You weigh yourself before a big meal—and after you've eaten and purged it—and discover that you haven't gained any weight, and perhaps have even lost a bit due to the amount of fluids you've purged. If you've vomited, the rush you get from noting the sensation of physical emptiness is enough to offset any initial disgust. If you overdosed on laxatives, the incorrect idea that you might not have gained anything from your binge helps you ignore the discomfort of the resulting explosive diarrhea. You pay no attention to the muscle weakness and lightheadedness that seems to follow any use of a diuretic.

You binge and purge on several more occasions, and it becomes easier to discount the physical side effects. Your initial feelings of revulsion or fear are soon replaced by the compulsion to repeat these behaviors; after a while you stop thinking logically about what you're doing. You just feel like you *have* to do it. You're hooked.

> *Sometimes when I purge I go at it point-blank and do it and I don't even consider my emotions. It's often just habit, an instant fix; I don't have to care about anything for the time being and I can move on with my life. I know that without it, I'll look and feel bad tomorrow. If I were honest, I'd admit that with it, I look and feel bad, today.*
>
> – Sara P., age 15

At this point, your life changes. Bingeing becomes the focus of your energies. You may find yourself thinking about food when you first awaken in the morning. You may try to organize your activities so that a certain amount of time is left free for bingeing. Your urge is probably strongest on days when you're particularly bored, tense, angry, or depressed. You may find that you *need* that binge to be able to move from one aspect of your day to another, such as from school to home life, or to mark the transition from work to relaxation.

Right before you actually begin a binge, you'll probably experience feelings of tension and anxiety, perhaps have heart palpitations and break into a sweat. It's important to recognize these physical sensations. *Your body is alerting you to the probability that you're in a pre-binge state.*

A Graphic Description of a Bulimic Binge and Purge Episode (Caution: May Be Triggering)

What happens during a binge? To begin with, you may not even have been hungry when you started to eat. Nonetheless, you'll consume an enormous number of calories by the time you're done. Some people choose sugary, starchy foods or those that are relatively high in fats. Others opt for smooth, milky foods like ice creams and puddings that can be easily vomited. So-called junk foods are usually preferred. One estimate says that an average binge ranges between 1,200 and 11,500 calories per binge; another estimate asserts that food intake can reach 166 calories per minute in a large binge.

Soon after starting the binge, you enter a "bulimic zone" and lose touch with your body and your surroundings. At this point, there's little chance that you'll taste or savor anything other than those initial bites of food. The physical act of eating the food during a binge is often mechanical—chew, swallow, chew, swallow. You will probably ignore the painful sensations you're apt to get when your stomach becomes distended and in distress.

> **Over time, you may lose the ability to tell when your body is hungry or full, and will have to relearn this after you stop being bulimic.**

The binge continues until no more food remains, the pain in your stomach becomes severe enough to get your attention, or an outside interruption (a phone call, ringing doorbell, barking dog, someone coming into your space) breaks into your bulimic zone.

Here's a letter I received that describes a bulimic binge:

Dear Nancy,

You need to warn people about the shock of a binge. You begin to eat and it feels great. You think you're getting away with something. You taste stuff, but only for a few minutes. Then the food feels like it is invading your mouth, like it doesn't belong there, like it will choke you. Sweet stuff stops tasting like anything. Crunchy and smooth become slimy and harsh, and swallowing becomes automatic but somehow difficult. You want to gag at times, after you can't taste, but you'll be doing that later, so you resist the urge. You don't want to eat anymore because your stomach hurts so much and there is tension at the base of your neck. You are in a total fog, almost like a blackout, yet you are wary, always wary of getting caught. Finally, you can't do it anymore and you push your-self away from the food, knowing that it will lure you back, again and again. But not now. Later, later...

Sincerely, Sylvey

Next comes the purge. Vomiting is initially very hard to do. People use different techniques to trigger the gag reflex and all-too-soon the behavior becomes routine. It is *never* acceptable to use an implement of any kind to make yourself vomit: to do so adds an element of danger to an already health-endangering process.

As an alternative or adjunct to vomiting, many bulimics take laxatives, diet pills, or emetics immediately after a binge since the fantasy is that this will cause weight loss. However, as the bulimia continues, you will have to take bigger doses to get the results you initially had: water loss, diminished hunger, the sense that you've "cleaned out" your system. This escalation of abuse is exactly what happens if you're addicted to alcohol or drugs.

Physical and Emotional Hazards of Bulimia

Bingeing followed by purging is extremely hazardous to your physical health. Taking emetics like ipecac is literally putting poison into your body, and you know that poison can kill. Misuse of ephedra-based supplements contributes to heart attack and strokes. In extreme instances, vomiting can cause your stomach to rupture (burst open). It can also cause something called *alkalosis*, which involves chemical changes in your blood resulting in a loss of calcium in your system, as well as tingling in your fingers, *tetany* (a series of uncomfortable muscle spasms in various body parts, often the legs), and damage to your liver, lungs, and heart. The acid in your stomach that is a component of the vomit can burn your esophagus, cause scar tissue to form, destroy the enamel of your teeth and create sores inside your mouth.

Repeated laxative abuse is a dangerous and misguided practice. It can destroy your bowel function and leave you with perpetual diarrhea and rectal bleeding. It can also deplete the sodium and potassium levels in your system (as do diuretics), which can then cause your heart to beat irregularly. In extreme cases, it can lead to heart failure, which can kill you. Ironically, laxatives don't really cause weight loss because they act on the lower portion of the gut, and calories are absorbed higher up. Also, laxatives produce watery stools, and any resulting weight loss is due to a loss of water.

If you misuse diuretics, you may find you have a lot of swelling in your body, especially noticeable in your fingers. This is a condition called *idiopathic edema* and it is most common in young women. It's uncomfortable, makes you think you're fat when in fact you're just swollen, and perpetuates an urge to purge because of the way you mistakenly read a body signal. You may find that your legs react to this self-imposed physical abuse: due to the loss of potassium in your system, they might throb, hurt when you put stress on them, or have little or no strength to support you even in the simplest act of walking.

If you're female, bulimia can cause menstrual irregularity, but a study done at the University of Minnesota Medical School has found that bulimia appears to have *no* long-term impact on a woman's ability to become pregnant (*American Journal of Psychiatry 2002; 159:1048-1050*).

Early into a binge you may feel free and less tense, but by the time you conclude a binge and begin the purging, that easing of tension can give way to feelings of guilt about what you've done. You might experience a lot of negative self-talk, a sense of hopelessness and resignation that there is no alternative but to yield to the purge, a belief that you're "bad," "worthless," and deserve the self-punishment of the purge. Those negative, uncomfortable feelings will lead to more tension, and then the conditions which gave rise to the cycle in the first place will begin again.

The Impact of Bulimia on Your Daily Routines and Relationships

When you are bulimic, food becomes like a narcotic and some "junk" foods seem irresistible. You have difficulty going into a grocery store, quick-shop, or bakery because you lack impulse control. You probably over-spend on binge foods and find it hard to get through a checkout line without tearing open one of the packages of food you're about to buy. You may go from place to place repeating the buy-eat pattern, scarfing down food in your car as you drive in search of more.

> **The more often you binge and purge, the more your routine will change to accommodate the compulsion.**

Bulimia also changes your relationships with others. It makes you afraid to eat anywhere with family or friends because you don't have confidence that you can control the urge to binge, or because you're no longer capable of eating anything, even if it isn't part of a binge, without having to purge it immediately afterwards. If you keep your bulimia a secret buried deep inside you, without admitting it to family and friends, that secrecy becomes another barrier, which separates you from the very people who could help you.

The purging is a turn-off. People may be willing to make excuses for quirky eating habits or even overlook them, but once you get into a pattern of excusing yourself from the table and returning from the bathroom looking blotchy, pale, or smelling of vomit, the social nature of sharing a meal with you changes. People may become edgy around you; you may sense an excessive amount of scrutiny from them. In some situations, your presence may no longer be desired because the dynamic around eating is one of tension, arguments, and turmoil. This discomfort can lead to a chain of events in which your family or friends avoid you, you avoid them, you isolate and feel like an outcast, and escalate the bulimia as the way to cope. (There is a certain irony in this because often bulimia is a way to fill emotional voids, described as "emptiness.")

Things at home (or school if you live away from home) can go from bad to worse. Your purging starts to impinge on the family or group turf: the bathrooms reek, the toilets are never completely clean, bed linens become soiled if you lose control of your bowels or vomit into a receptacle while you're in or on your bed, and the food you're hoarding under the bed or in closets spoils and attracts insects. You may even start stealing money from friends or relatives to support your food habit. At this stage, you can lose the sympathy of your family or roommates, and your bulimic behaviors spark tremendous anger in them. Even though everyone feels the anger, it's unlikely that you'd discuss it openly or honestly. They may not understand why you're doing these things, and they may become frightened when they see you're out of control.

> Marilyn had been my roommate since we started boarding school in ninth grade. By the middle of our junior year she'd become like a stranger to me. She started pilfering small amounts of money from my purse, thinking I didn't notice, and then she snitched my silver ring. Her appearance got sloppier, and she had a body odor I couldn't pinpoint. I could feel a kind of rage inside me almost every morning, and she seemed totally unaware of how I was feeling about her. I didn't have the nerve to confront her. It was only when I caught her vomiting and saw she had also downed a whole box of Ex-Lax in the bathroom that I put two and two together. I got our housemother, who called her parents. Marilyn hates me for it.
>
> – Pammy K., age 17

Because people with bulimia don't always look emaciated, chances are you'll get tougher treatment from your family than you would if you looked as if you were anorexic. If you steadfastly refuse to try to change, or if you're so far enmeshed in the bulimic patterns that you *can't* make changes without professional help, people may misinterpret your actions. They may forget that this is about you and your struggle with an illness, and instead think that you're purposely trying to hurt, embarrass, or "dis" them. Your bulimia comes across as a slap in the face.

Sadly, some families who try to make sense of the bulimia without fully understanding what's happening and without talking about it directly, openly, and honestly to one another end up involved in some domestic abuse, as if strong-arming you would help you "come to your senses." You may find that you're actually being slapped around or verbally assaulted. There can be irate yelling, blaming, and shaming; sometimes a bulimic family member is asked to leave home and stay somewhere else.

> *Now that I'm better, I can feel for my parents. I guess they really had no other option but to throw me out. I was destroying our family life. I'd vomit each time I ate anything, and I couldn't hide what I was doing from my little sister. She got so scared of me that she refused to sit in the same room with me alone. Her teacher told my mom that my sister's schoolwork was going downhill. I guess I was the cause. My mom and dad fought over me all the time. It was like living in hell. I left and got picked up by a juvenile officer. That's what brought me into therapy. Thank goodness it worked.*
>
> *– Yolanda B., age 18*

It's hard to be bulimic—the physical and emotional tolls are tremendous. It's also hard *not* to be bulimic once you've fallen into the binge-purge habit. But change is possible and even though it is often a process of successes, setbacks, realizations and resolutions unique to each individual, recovery from bulimia is worth all the time and effort involved.

Ten Things to Remember about Bulimia

1. Bulimia is a pattern in which you binge (eat a huge amount of food in a short period of time) and then purge (eliminate) whatever you ate.

2. Bulimia is a self-destructive activity that makes it almost impossible to eat in a normal, unselfconscious way.

3. Bulimic "hunger" is most often emotionally driven, binges and purges provide release but not pleasure, food becomes an antagonist, and eating is disconnected from physical and emotional nourishment.

4. Bulimic binges and purges are habit-forming and become intense, negative forces that dominate your life and are hazardous to your emotional and physical health.

5. Bulimia is more prevalent than anorexia but is harder to detect because many bulimics are not obviously underweight and do not seem to restrict what they eat.

6. Sometimes it's difficult to know if a person is really bulimic or has a form of anorexia that involves bingeing and purging. An accurate diagnosis from a health-care professional is needed to ensure the right kind of treatment.

7. Bulimia may surface after someone has battled anorexia.

8. Although many people struggle in secret, estimates suggest that between 1 and 5% of adolescent and college-age women in the U.S. are bulimic; between 10 and 20% of bulimic patients are male.

9. Bulimia can be a learned behavior picked up in the context of a certain kind of family or peer group situation.

10. Bulimia often coexists in a person with other problems such as depression, anxiety, social phobia, seasonal affective disorder, drug or alcohol abuse, or cutting.

PART II

Eating Disorders Recovery

chapter six

First Steps Toward Recovery

"An eating disorder! It was so hard to admit. I didn't want that label. I was mad that I was found out. Sometimes I want help, while at other times I don't."

— Della J., age 15

One of the toughest aspects of being a teenager or young adult is wanting everyone to think you've got your act together when you're also struggling with questions like, "Who am I?" "What do I want to do with my life?" "Does anyone really love me?" "Will I ever be happy?" "Will I be a success?" "How can I be everything that everyone expects me to be?" and so on. It's hard to maintain a veneer of competence when you're thinking, "I suck at life." While there are many factors that contribute to the development of an eating disorder, this uncertainty about who you are and what you stand for can make you particularly susceptible.

For this reason, the first steps that you need to take in overcoming your eating disorder involve getting to know yourself and your unique situation. This includes examining your discomforts and dissatisfactions with the "reality" of your life. Although it can be difficult, at first, to pinpoint the reasons why an eating disorder is part of that reality, anorexia and bulimia almost always start out with behaviors and thoughts that have pattern and logic, and are voluntary and under your control. As such, they *can* be overcome. In order to fight them though, you need to understand about eating disorders (which you do if you've read this far) and then apply that information to your life by acknowledging the disorder's role in it, and taking appropriate steps toward change.

These first steps toward recovery are probably the most important ones you'll take. They require the willingness to take an honest look at your life, the courage to describe it accurately, and the desire to find out what your eating disorder does *to* you and *for* you. After that, you'll have a good idea of what to put in its place that is more positive and life-enhancing.

> **What you'll choose to change will depend on your unique set of circumstances, your goals, the time frame you set for yourself, and your motivation.**

A number of tools can help you get comfortable with this initial process of recovery, some of which you may already know about, such as journal writing, taking relaxation breaks, and cultivating relationships with people you trust and enjoy. Other steps will probably be new to you, such as "taking dictation from yourself" by answering deeply personal questions; noting, challenging and changing your negative self-talk and negative triggers; and defusing your eating environment one step at a time to help you begin thinking about food and eating in non-eating-disordered ways. Eventually, you'll change how you respond to and communicate with people so the eating disorder won't have to do that for you. In addition, your "world view" that thinness determines your personal worth will shift, and you'll rebuild self-esteem on a more secure foundation.

Getting Motivated

It can be tough to get motivated to do all this soul searching and make life changes, especially if you think your eating disorder isn't that serious. You may not yet perceive (much less believe) that your physical and emotional well-being are impaired or at risk. What's worse, since anorexia and bulimia can start out as behaviors that seem "normal" and acceptable in our culture, you might be rationalizing your early symptoms by saying things like,

- "Being thin is healthy."
- "A lot of exercise is better than no exercise."
- "I'm fine!"
- "Everybody diets."

It *is* true that a majority of women, and an increasing number of men, are compelled to diet and exercise, often to the extreme, in order to be thin. They mistakenly believe that thinness will guarantee them health, happiness, success, love and any number of other goals. They spend an incredible amount of time, money, and energy going on (and off) diets, regaining the weight, wondering what went wrong, and repeating the process again and again.

In fact, these people share with you similar patterns of thinking and behaving, although theirs may not be as extreme or potentially life-threatening as yours. Just like you, they believe that thinness will solve their problems. Their lives, like yours, revolve around what they eat or don't eat, how much they weigh, and what other people think of them.

> **But whether you are "just" a dieter or have symptoms of a full-blown eating disorder, you are still living in a prison of restriction and low self-esteem.**

You shouldn't have to walk around every day secretly hating your body because you've bought into our culture's relentless conection between low weight and self-worth. *Just because our culture condones this focus doesn't make it right.*

So, be prepared for the possibility that those initial steps meant to liberate you from the prison of your eating disorder will be tentative, shaky, and scary. You'll have to examine and challenge this drive for thinness, be willing to eat properly, exercise appropriately, honor your body's need for sleep, and come to terms with your body's natural shape. You might have to change friends if yours are obsessed with weight loss, or teach them what you're learning as you resolve the issues that landed you in this prison. You'll have to be willing to talk with your family and, eventually, your therapy team, about the changes going on inside your head.

Whether you're being pressured into recovery by outside influences, like a parent or friend who's on your case, or whether you're initiating change on your own, remember that your goal is to be finally free from an obsession that has millions of other people stuck.

> **Applaud yourself for having the courage to change.**

Also, recognize and try to accept that it will take some time before you'll be free enough from food and weight fears to be able to fully appreciate and care for the miracle that is your own body. But you will, and when that happens, every step that led you there will have been worth the effort.

> *"Recovery is a fluid state, not a fixed point...if you push through, you move into its center, where you find that the state of recovery is an ongoing effort of major proportions, and with enormous rewards."*
>
> – Marya Hornbacher (author of *Wasted*)

Self-Awareness Starts With Writing About Yourself

How well do you know yourself? People with eating disorders are often unnecessarily and inaccurately self-critical. That tendency needs to change if recovery is to occur, and that means becoming self-aware. Start the process by taking "dictation from yourself" and answering the following questions in a journal or notebook. No one will see what you have written without your permission, so be honest!

Initial Writing Exercise

1. What are ten things you like about yourself?
2. What are ten things you don't like about yourself?
3. Which list took longer to write?
4. Which list do you feel most convinced about? Why?
5. What is your definition of "happiness?"
6. What is your definition of "control?"
7. Who or what makes you feel terific? When? Why?
8. Who or what makes you feel awful? When? Why?

Now, let's delve a little deeper to uncover more specific issues, beliefs, or situations that may underlie your eating disorder. Think of yourself as an archaeologist at a dig where you are both the investigator and one being investigated!

> **Try to see yourself objectively,**
> **without judgement or blame.**

Be as detailed as possible in your search. Pay attention to influences that you previously may have overlooked, forgotten, or refused to acknowledge. Are there repetitive themes in your thinking?

Are any patterns emerging? Can you begin to see why you have certain feelings and beliefs about food and eating, and why you behave in certain ways around them?

This self-awareness is the basis for the strategy you, and eventually your support team, will create to handle each of the influences that trigger, escalate, and perpetuate your unique eating-disordered pattern. Then you can alter or eliminate these influences gradually, one at a time, so that you're not overwhelmed and will be more likely to keep taking those steps toward recovery.

Do you feel in control of your life in general, and specifically where food and eating are concerned?

- What does your personal habit profile (from Chapter 3) look like?

- Are you or your habits in the driver's seat?

- Do you have freedom of choice about your life, or does it seem like you have to do what everyone else wants you to do?

- Do you have freedom of choice about what and how much you eat at home, or is yours a "clean your plate" family?

- Are you involved in the choosing and preparation of food?

Who and what influence you?

- Are there individuals or groups of people who routinely provoke your urge to binge, binge/purge, or strengthen your desire to diet?

- Has a coach, parent, or teacher ever pushed you to lose weight?

Is there a specific, *predictable, recurrent* event or situation that consistently triggers your urge to binge or strengthens your resolve to restrict your food intake?

- How do you react to media stories and media hype about diets, dieting, exercise, body-image, physical beauty, sexuality, etc?
- Do you have any idols or role models who are extremely or inappropriately thin?

What do you believe?

- Do you believe that losing weight and being thin are shortcuts to happiness and personal power?
- What is your definition of "personal power"?
- Do you equate food and eating with love and caring?
- Do you believe that preparing, serving, and eating food is a way to "control" others?

What is your typical communication style?

- Are you more likely to keep things to yourself, speak your mind with ease and confidence, or speak in half-truths?
- Do you use "I language" (i.e., "I need to know your opinion." "I feel so angry right now.") and state your position clearly, even if it's unpopular or emotionally revealing?
- Do you prefer to negotiate instead of fighting?
- Do you argue for the sake of arguing?
- Do you give in easily even though you think you're right?

What do you do in your spare time?

- Do you participate in a sport or other activity (such as ballet) for which a low weight is required?

- Do you like doing things alone more than you like doing things as part of a group?

- Do you make a distinction between solitude and isolation?

- Can you be alone with yourself and not feel lonely?

How aware are you of your eating habits?

- Is there a typical pattern between moments of stress in your life and your eating urges?

- Is there a particular time of day or night when you're most in need of a binge?

- Who or what prompts your need to restrict?

- What is it about eating that feels threatening to you?

- Did something happen in your life to make certain foods scary or safe?

Taking Inventory

Once you've finished with these self-awareness questions, it's helpful to organize what you've learned about yourself in chart form, such as the "personal inventory" in the following example. In your case, you're taking inventory of and making decisions about people, things, and situations that affect your feelings and attitudes about food and eating as well as about your self-image and self-esteem. It will help you clarify the "ABCs" of your anorexia and/or bulimia: Antecedents, or what came before; Behaviors, or what is happening now; and Consequences, or results. Mark anyone or anything that was or has been *positive* with a "+" and conversely, the *negative* influences with a "−".

My Personal Inventory

Who?	When?	What and/or Where?	Why?	Still?
Mom (+)	always	family dinners	she listens to me	yes, is a help
Dad (−)	always	weekend meals at Grandma's	criticizes me, calls me "chub," and watches me eat	yes, even though I'm thin now
Coach (−)	practice	school	says I'm too thin, too weak to be goalie	yes
Ballet teacher (−)	always	class	sets impossible goals for our bodies, I never feel good enough	yes
Boyfriend (+)	always	school and at his house	his house is the only place where I feel safe eating; no one watches me, I feel in control there	yes
Best friend (−)	since junior year	school, at parties	says I'm impossible, is jealous of me	yes
	after school	teen magazines (+,−)	make me wish I looked like a model, (−) but teach me a lot (+)	yes

Isolating Your Negative Triggers

Your personal inventory should yield a clear picture of many factors that have created the "necessary and sufficient" conditions for an eating disorder to become part of your life—in other words, your negative triggers. Most likely, these are the items you marked with the minus signs. They are called triggers because they operate like the trigger on a pistol, which has to be activated before the bullet can be shot and damage done. So it is with eating disorder triggers: once they're activated, anorexic or bulimic behaviors get released and do damage—to you.

Negative triggers can take many forms, and often more than one is at work. Words that are said to you, looks people give you, being in uncomfortable situations with certain individuals, can all be triggers. They make you react intensely (though you don't usually admit it), and probably feel as though you're constantly "ducking:" defensive, down, anxious, uncomfortable, unhappy, vulnerable, depressed, and in need of some kind of protection. Once activated, these triggers lead to anorexic or bulimic behaviors, which then become your "armor." Here are some examples.

My swimming coach spent years telling everyone on the team to keep our weight down, and he could be counted on to yell each time anybody gained a few pounds. Every time I heard the opening lines of his speech, "Girls, it's apparent you're not serious about the shape you have to be in . . ." I got a knot in my stomach and broke out into cold chills even when the temperature at the pool was hot. Every time that happened, I'd go home and binge and then have to vomit and I didn't see the connection until recently.

– Bettina H., age 17

I think my eating disorder did originate at home with my parents. But it wasn't that they wanted me to "clean my plate."

No, in our house my mother is a health fanatic and makes substitute low-calorie foods. I thought it would be wonderful to have been in a family that wanted me to eat. I was embarrassed to be hungry in my house and I knew my mother really wanted me to diet. I felt my parents watching exactly how much I ate, and the pressure started there.

– Janine K., age 18

Negative triggers are totally personal, although many people have similar triggers, even identical ones. Concern yourself only with those that are problematic for *you*, especially if you're in the habit of comparing notes with other anorexics and bulimics, or if your friends and relatives are in the habit of telling you what your problems are. Trust yourself. Review your answers to the self-awareness and personal inventory sections of this chapter. Break things down into their smaller parts; look for cause-effect patterns. The process can be hit-or-miss. Try to take it one step at a time and don't expect instant "ahas!" These written exercises buy you time to think, give you a focus for discussing issues with the relevant people, and increase your ability to exert some control by getting actively involved in airing and solving what you perceive to be problematic.

Defusing Your Eating Environment One Step at a Time

After you've identified your negative triggers, the next step is to defuse your eating environment, one step at a time. Again, this has to be an individualized, personal exercise because no two people are alike, and also because what you'll need to do if you're anorexic is likely to be different from what you'll need to do if you're bulimic.

One question that anyone in recovery from an eating disorder should answer is, "What can I or can't I tolerate?" We all have limits. If you *know* what or how much you can eat, with whom you eat, and where you eat before you reach a point at which the anorexic or bulimic patterns get triggered, you can establish a baseline—a safety zone—that you can try to duplicate each time you have to deal with food. Then you can build on this baseline and extend it gradually. Try to think logically and analytically about the foods that you either eat or don't eat, "safe" foods versus "fear" foods, foods you find pleasurable and digestible versus those you believe you must purge or restrict.

Does the odor of a particular food or combination of foods play any part in your eating disorder?

If so, try to change that. Experiment with different foods, keeping in mind that a balanced diet is imperative for your health. Try to desensitize yourself. For instance, you might place scented candles on the dining table to add contrasting aromas and give you a focal point other than the food. The idea is that you are defusing the negative trigger of the food *odor,* and replacing it with a different set of responses that won't be typical anorexic or bulimic ones.

Does the visual impact of food or combination of foods play any part in your eating disorder?

Some people can't stand to look at meats; others need to organize their foods in particular patterns on a plate; some can tolerate only tiny amounts on a plate at any one time. Again, try to change the power that the food on the plate has over you. Experiment. Pretend to be an artist working on a canvas. Change things around till you find a food or combination of foods that won't trigger anorexic or bulimic patterns. If you can get into the mind game of imagining yourself as an artist with the food as your medium, you might be able to distract or amuse yourself enough so that some of the emotional punch associated with food will be eliminated and you'll be able to eat with greater ease.

Does the taste of any particular food or combination of foods play any part in your eating disorder?

Each of us has food preferences, and it's natural that some foods trigger more intense reactions than others. Problems can occur when you don't have the chance to let your personal sense of taste influence what you eat. Have people in your family always eaten their food cooked with certain spices or to a certain degree of doneness and given you no choice in the matter? Are you particularly sensitive to sweet, salt, sour, or bitter tastes? Do you have food allergies? Do certain tastes repulse you and make it impossible for you to eat anything at all? It's important to explore these questions because your solution may be a simple one: substitute similarly nutritious foods for the ones you can't stand.

If you don't know much about food and nutrition, chances are that whatever you do know includes some misinformation. Most of us believe the things we hear and read in food advertisements, which put a spin on their sales pitches. For example, we're often led to believe that fat-free or low-fat foods are the healthiest choices. What we aren't told is that such food products make up for the bland flavors (due to the lower fat content) by including a host of other additives.

Since educating yourself is a major part of the recovery process, and correct nutritional information is extremely important, research a variety of sources and be skeptical about what you read. Ask the librarian in your school or public library to help you locate accurate books or pamphlets about nutrition; do online searches; speak to your family doctor; or make an appointment with a qualified nutritionist or licensed dietitian who is not affiliated with a food company or weight-control program that is trying to "sell" you something.

Does the location of the meal play any part in your eating-disordered thinking and behaving?

It's possible that you can eat in a relatively normal fashion in one location (like the dining room), but not in another (like the kitchen). Find a neutral, non-triggering place *that isn't isolated* and start there. We're not talking about alternative locales where you can feel comfortable bingeing and purging, or restricting. You might decide to eat your meals at a friend's house for a few days or weeks. You might ask your family if you could move in with a grandparent for a short period of time. Make certain your options are acceptable to your family. Gain confidence. The goal is to relearn the skill and pleasure of being able to eat *anywhere* with *anyone* and not need the eating disorder to help you do so.

Do you have any habits/rituals before, during, or after meals that play a part in your eating disorder?

Rituals are very important components of the eating disordered lifestyle. Whether the habits are arranging binge foods so they sit in a certain order on the table, setting up an actual barrier between yourself and whomever else you are eating with so they can't watch you eat, or cutting a single pea into tiny slivers, you should try to eliminate them. They isolate you by focusing your energy and attention on the eating process, energy that could be better used communicating with people you care about, doing things that are fun for you, and learning.

> **Caution: don't try to eliminate every habit and ritual at once; take it one step at a time.**

If you have to cut your food into pieces, try to cut fewer pieces. If you have to isolate yourself, set a kitchen timer and allow yourself those few minutes of solitude before you join the rest of the family. Gradually decrease your time alone. Buy fewer items for your binge; put away the money you save to reward yourself for your successes. As the preventive tactics start to work, you'll find your rituals aren't as necessary as you think.

(Note: some people's rituals are so intense that a clinical diagnosis of "obsessive-compulsive disorder" is made. If you think you need to be evaluated to see if you might have this disorder, talk to a psychiatrist. If the diagnosis is made, there are medications that can be prescribed to help alleviate the obsessions and compulsions.)

Are there any habits/rituals that other people you eat with frequently engage in before, during, or after meals, which play a part in your eating disorder?

Perhaps your grandmother who lives with you belches loudly during meals as a way of showing her satisfaction, and you think it's gross. Perhaps your father smokes a smelly cigar before and after dinner, but that rattles your taste buds and your sense of smell. Your little brother chews with his mouth wide open and seems to do it just to annoy you. Maybe your mother won't sit down to eat until everyone else is served or spends the time she should be dining with you doing dishes and grumbling about it. Mealtimes are therefore filled with tension.

Things of this sort can be eating disorder triggers. You might want to discuss your reactions with whoever's involved by suggesting alternatives and negotiating. This can be awkward, especially if you're talking with someone who might take offense.

> Regardless of the results, any positive attempt you make to express your feelings strengthens your voice.

You might try to understand why things are as they are. Can you see any humor in the situation? Can you feel compassion for those people who seem to be caught in their own automatic behaviors?

Do you have any recurring fears or fantasies about certain foods or combinations of foods that play a part in your eating disorder?

You may worry about a food's effect on you. You may have inaccurate notions about what will happen if you allow yourself to eat specific ones, like: you'll instantly put on weight all over your body; you'll develop fat thighs; your face will become bloated; you'll start a binge; people will think you're weak-willed. Perhaps you've developed a system of "safe" and "unsafe" foods that let you get through mealtimes and feel okay about yourself, but usually those safe foods aren't nutritionally appropriate and don't provide enough calories and nutrients to keep you healthy.

Following are a few ideas to help you overcome these fears and fantasies about food.

Facing Food Fears: A Food Hierarchy

Although facing food fears without the help of a therapist or other caregiver can be difficult, you *can* do a few things on your own to develop more realistic and accurate thoughts and feelings about food. One strategy is to create a *food hierarchy,* such as the one below, which will help you see what you're avoiding. Once you've written down the names of foods and categorized them, it's difficult to deny what you've been thinking and how you've been behaving regarding them. This will make you accountable to yourself.

Divide a piece of notebook paper into four horizontal sections with the top one labeled "Safest Foods" (or "Least Forbidden Foods"), followed by "Somewhat Forbidden Foods," "Extremely Forbidden Foods," and "Unsafe Foods" (or "Most Forbidden Foods"). Fill in each section. You may be surprised to discover that the foods you list as "unsafe" are actually foods you used to prefer and even ate with pleasure (instead of with guilt or fear) such as French fries, pizza, fried chicken, or chocolate cake.

Safest – Least Forbidden _____

_____

Somewhat Forbidden _____

_____

Extremely Forbidden _____

_____

Unsafe – Most Forbidden_____

_____

What do you do with this information? Use the hierarchy to help you gradually relearn to eat appropriate amounts of foods that you've listed in the "forbidden" categories. Every time you succeed in moving a food up through the ranks of the hierarchy until it's among your safe foods, you are that much closer to loosening the bonds of your eating disorder.

Another way to defuse food fears is to honestly answer the question, "What's the worst possible thing that will happen to me if I let myself eat this food?" Chances are nothing earth-shattering will happen (presuming you're not allergic to the food). Your body will NOT immediately become fat (although this might be your foremost fear), your personality won't change, your I.Q. won't plummet, and your friends won't disappear. Your family won't break up just because you ate something you were afraid to eat or thought you shouldn't. If you do a reality check, you'll see that all you've done is add "fuel" (nutrients) to your "engine" (body).

Relaxation exercises are also an effective way to handle food fears, especially right before you eat. Visualize (imagine) yourself in a pleasurable and happy situation. *Feel* the sensations that go along with your imagery. Try to savor whatever positive sensations emerge and let them calm you. Or, try listening to soothing music before a meal. Take a leisurely bath. Go for a walk (but not a power-walk to burn calories, nor a run). Call a friend. Snuggle with your pet. Read a good book.

> **Put yourself into a pleasurable situation so the good feelings it engenders can be taken with you when you sit down to eat the particular food.**

A Blueprint for Positives

Another helpful step in early recovery is to develop a vision for the life you imagine living without the eating disorder, or at least with it in check. Once you decide to be the architect of your own recovery and create your own "blueprint" for change, you're in a position to recognize that eating-disordered choices and behaviors are *not* ordinary and natural. They're dangerous and self-destructive.

Here are some suggestions.

1. Don't try to build a castle before you've had the chance to build a hut.

This means that your blueprint should start out simple. Small steps are fine. Pick out one or two tasks to defuse the negative triggers *you* really want to work on and think you can conquer. For instance, eat one non-eating-disordered meal per weekend with the family or limit what you buy in preparation for a binge. Perhaps when something is making you uncomfortable and is triggering you, clearly state what's wrong *in the moment* to the person whose behavior is problematic. Keep at it until the individual tasks you've selected no longer trigger an eating-disordered response. You will gain skills and self-confidence to take on more complex tasks that will, in turn, release you from more and more triggers.

2. Revise your blueprint every few weeks.

Give yourself a *reasonable* time period to try your preventive strategies that is neither too short nor too long. This way, you'll be working within a framework of success rather than failure. If things aren't going well, you can reset your goals and strategies and begin anew. If things go well, however, you'll be surprised at how quickly you were able to reverse old habits and revise your point of view. Pat yourself on the back for your accomplishments and turn your attention to a new set of goals to help loosen the grip of the eating disorder.

3. Every architect has colleagues. Decide who yours will be and establish ground rules for your relationships with them.

Now is the time to start thinking about "coming out" with your secret and getting help from other people. Initially, this might be a friend or member(s) of your family, a school counselor or pastor at your place of worship. Further down the road, you may need the added help of a therapist or therapy team.

You want to choose individuals you trust enough to take your situation seriously, with whom you can imagine yourself "agreeing to disagree" if your points-of-view differ, clash, and change as your relationships evolve. These might be people who are part of your problem (or not) but who are willing to act as your sounding board and honestly answer the question, "How am I doing?" You might want to tell a lot of people what you're trying to accomplish, or just a few. The key is to be prepared to have *someone* to confide in as you implement your preventive strategies, because you need multiple perspectives to challenge your own.

In order to encourage productive communication, establish ground rules for each of these relationships. Do you want the other person to initiate a discussion of how things are coming along, or do *you* want to be the one to do so? Are you willing to discuss things at any time, or do you prefer a certain time of day or night? Do you want to be informal, or do you want to actually make appointments for these discussions? Ground rules like these help you get the most out of your discussions, especially in the early stages of recovery when your own communicative skills may need honing and when you will need to acknowledge that your viewpoint is not always the correct one.

A final word about ground rules that might be hard for you to accept right now. If you have been hanging out with "friends" who have functioned as your binge buddies by encouraging you to diet excessively, or who have been bulimia "pushers" by pressuring you to entice others to try what you've all been doing with food, *you must change the rules of those relationships* if you plan to stay friends with them. In practical terms, this means that you might need to tell them things like, "I'm not doing any binges with you from now on and don't try to change my mind," or "I don't want to talk about the latest laxatives and diet drinks or pills anymore," or "I'm not going to compare our weights each morning with you." Then tell them why.

> **Friends who care about you and who are interested in helping you regain your health will listen and try to accommodate you.**

But if they seem angry and try to make you feel it's you who's being unreasonable, *don't feel guilty, and don't back down.* Sometimes you have to face up to the fact that such people may not be true friends.

4. Keep a weekly log.

A weekly log helps you track the thoughts, behaviors, and situations you either have or haven't changed, and then evaluate why. It helps you decide what to work on, assess when you've achieved a particular goal, and choose what to tackle next. Try using the following format:

Recovery Task (*describe it*)

Goal (*describe it*)

What has to be done to achieve the goal?
(*list the elements involved*)

Days the task is carried out (*write the actual date*)

How did it go?

Risks (*list them even if you think they're just in your imagination*)

Gains (*list them*)

Needs further work*? ("Yes"* or *"No")*

Goal achieved? (*"Yes"* or *"No"*)

5. Evaluate your success at least once a week.

Get into the habit of taking credit for your successes. Focus on the positives. Talk with the people who are in this with you and get their opinions of your successes. Chances are they'll see even more than you do.

Although these first steps in recovery demand a lot of work on your part, the payoff is immeasurable. Your goal is to be free of food and weight fears and to love your body and your self in order to live a joyful and productive life. What could be more worthwhile?

Ten Details About Your First Steps Toward Recovery

1. An important objective of those first steps is to pinpoint why your eating disorder occurs, persists, and becomes powerful.

2. It takes a lot of courage to be honest enough to do this.

3. Your first steps are likely to be tentative and shaky. Even if you're scared, one challenge is to take the steps no matter what.

4. When you make an inventory of the people, things, and situations that you believe contribute to your eating disorder, you will have a lot of important information to share with your treatment team.

5. Isolating your negative triggers will help you understand the logic of your eating disorder and change its patterns.

6. Relearning to eat and think about food in a non-eating-disordered way takes time, patience, and a strategy that both makes sense and that you're willing to use.

7. One of the most challenging of the first steps is facing your food fears.

8. A food hierarchy will clarify which foods you fear the most and help you overcome those fears.

9. Relaxation and visualization techniques help you take the first steps towards recovery with more confidence and less tension.

10. A blueprint for the life you imagine living without the eating disorder (or with it in check) will connect you to a positive goal. Revise it every few weeks as you gain confidence in the process of change.

chapter seven

"Coming Out"

When Your Secret Is an Eating Disorder

"I don't mean this as a pun: when I told my parents about the eating disorder, a big weight was lifted from me. The kind that has nothing to do with 'weight.'"

— Janine P., age 16

Being honest with yourself, about yourself, can be difficult; sharing that honesty with others can be even more difficult. An eating disorder is the kind of secret you'd probably like to keep to yourself, especially if you're worried that opening up would make you feel insecure, embarrassed or threatened. Both anorexia and bulimia layer self-destructive habits over your otherwise ordinary routines, and in general, the more layers there are, the greater is your need for secrecy and the more intense is your denial that there is a problem. You may even get lulled into a false belief that your anorexia and/or bulimia *can* remain hidden forever. They can't.

When Others Try to Get You to Give Up Your Eating Disorder

Often, people figure out that you have a problem without being told. Your symptoms may be dramatic and trigger intense reactions in them. Some worry and tell you so. Others are intimidated and frightened, unsure how to respond, especially when you're in an eating-disordered mode. Some will speak to you out of concern or frustration because they care for and about you. Others will want to "correct" your thinking or "cure" your eating disorder, without really knowing how.

A battleground mentality can set in. The eating disorder becomes the enemy, you are its victim, and the other person (e.g., a parent, friend, relative, or teacher) becomes your helper or "rescuer." Typically, several people will confront you about your eating habits, so it's possible to have many would-be rescuers. Some won't know specifically that what you have is an eating disorder and won't use technically correct terms to describe what they think you're doing. They may say, "You're too thin" or "You're not taking care of yourself." People who are well-informed may try logic and offer facts about the dangers to your physical and mental health.

When those arguments don't result in the desired changes in your behavior, rescuers may also try to shake you up with threats of dire consequences like, "You'll lose all your friends," "You won't be allowed to continue living with us," or "You'll end up in the hospital." They might try a guilt-trip technique like, "Look what you're doing to us," "If you cared about anyone else, you wouldn't do this," or "You're so selfish." They might abandon the "logic" approach, become emotional, and beg you to stop such self-destruction. They may literally bribe you:

> *My parents made a deal with me that if I got my period before my birthday, they'd get me a car and I could choose the color. This is one example of the bribes this eating disorder has brought out. Some of the others include a shopping spree if I have my period three months in a row. I think you get the point. It makes me sad that my parents think of me as such a shallow person that I could be cured from my eating disorder by some simple bribing.*
>
> – Kaye H., age 15

If you're *not* ready to accept someone else's help, if you feel protected by your eating disorder and have no interest in listening to the other person's point-of-view, any attempt at changing your mind can feel like a power struggle, with one person trying to take control and the other feeling powerless. One unintended consequence of this power struggle may be that the grip of the eating disorder is actually *strengthened*. External pressure to change something that is such an important part of your identity can make you even more stubborn in your resolve to keep the status quo. You might even realize how "stuck" you are, yet be totally resistant to change.

Trying to fend off your rescuers as you struggle to keep at least part of your secret intact may lead to some very frustrating, angry, and emotionally draining conversations. You may not realize it, but you are defending a series of behaviors and thoughts that the other person finds indefensible.

The following responses are typical of anorexics and bulimics who *aren't* ready to give up their eating disorders, followed by some possible alternatives:

Response #1:

"That's definitely not me."

You are telling others that they're misinterpreting your behavior. However, this is usually not true and vehement denial won't necessarily get those people off your case. In fact, your denial may trigger stronger efforts to get you to acknowledge the seriousness of your situation.

Is it possible that you're scared to admit it *is* you, and that you're having trouble understanding what your behavior is all about?

Resonse #2:

"Everybody does it."

This is the safety-in-numbers, "it's socially acceptable" response. There may be some truth in this statement: many people do diet to extreme, and bingeing is common. But "everybody" does *not* do it.

If you *really* believe that your choices are "normal," you probably have an eating disorder as a constant companion.

Is it possible that you're exhausted by having to spend so much time and energy on your disorder, and that you would rather not be part of that particular crowd?

Response #3:

> *"It's part of my routine. I do it for me. It's my choice. It's a lifestyle thing like choosing a perfume or hair color or whether or not to wear deodorant."*

This rationalization characterizes your eating or dieting behavior as voluntary. You are trying to minimize, even trivialize, the importance of an eating disorder in your daily life. But if you have to deny, rationalize, or trivialize it this way, the eating disorder is no longer a matter of your free will and choice, but an addictive habit that is now in control of you.

Is is possible for you to acknowledge that your routine needs to be changed and that you need to ask for help in developing a plan for that change?

Response #4:

> *"I have to do it to . . . make the team/make the weight class/ keep in shape/feel good/be happy/etc."*

You desperately want others to see the "logic" behind your behavior to prove that it is rational, planned, and/or productive. What remains unsaid is the devastating impact it is probably having on your mental and physical health. Your reply invites the other person to bombard you with facts to challenge and disprove your "logic".

Is it possible for you to see that what may have worked for you in the past is harming you in the present?

Response #5:

> *"I'm not a druggie, so get off my case."*

An angry, confrontational response of this sort minimizes the seriousness of an eating disorder by saying you're not dabbling in something that "could" be worse, like taking illegal, addictive drugs. However, the person you address is likely to pick up the thread of your argument and weave in comparisons between eating disorders and drug addictions. Thus, you may inadvertently undermine your own position.

Is it possible for you to express how frustrated and angry you feel and begin a dialogue about that?

Response #6:

"It's my body, my business, my life."

Are you pleading the Fifth? It's obvious that you're attempting to short-circuit any further conversation. This won't work. What's more likely to happen is that whoever you're talking to will get more frustrated and angry than before you began the discussion and rather than trying to reason *with* you will start to talk *at* you.

Is it possible for you to talk about how you define "taking responsibility" for yourself and your health, and maybe even discuss how you and your family define "privacy?"

Response #7:

"If you stop watching me and treating me like I'm a baby . . .
I'll eat what you cook/eat dinner at the table with the family/
won't overdo the junk/etc."

You're right in one sense: it isn't fun to have every bite you eat monitored by someone else. But the "let's make a deal" tone of "if you do this, I'll do that" is just one of the game-playing techniques of the eating-disordered mind. These deals might work for a while, but in the long run everyone involved loses.

Is it possible for everyone in this situation to lay all their cards out on the table and work out a solution?

Why "Coming Out" Is Better than Being "Found Out"

If you have an eating disorder, it's better (though harder) to decide to "come out" of your own free will rather than be "found out" or confronted, as in the previous scenarios. This is because when you come out, *you're* taking charge. You're also giving permission for other people to help you deal with your eating disorder. When you come out, you may not be able to predict the upshot of your decision, but at least you, and the people with whom you have chosen to share your secret, can refocus your collective energies on recovery.

> **Having anorexia or bulimia isolates you from the people and events in your environment, so coming out may be the ultimate act of courage.**

It's a self-revelation that exposes the core of your vulnerability—the eating disorder—and gives other people the opportunity to understand and help. Coming out demystifies your secret, and allows them and you to assess the behaviors involved in anorexia and bulimia using non-eating-disordered logic. It proves you're willing to be in the spotlight, almost like an actor who is taking advice from a demanding director. You have to listen to another person whose spin on the situation is very different from your own, and probably learn things about yourself from that person. You may also need to change your actions and reactions according to the director's sense of your performance and progress.

Who will be your initial "director?" That depends upon the seriousness of your eating disorder and what effects it has had on your mental and physical health up to this point. Your director could be a doctor, therapist, nutritionist, or dietitian. It could be a parent, friend, teacher, or someone who has recovered from an eating disorder. Directors and rescuers can be the same people—the only differences have to do with your attitude towards them and your understanding of what it is they're trying to do for and with you.

There are no guarantees that coming out will be met with applause from your audience, so it's natural to wonder why you should even bother! The unknowns are risky and you may feel like the mythical Pandora who opened her box and let all life's ills and evils escape into the world. In reality, though, the risks are almost always offset by the rewards, and coming out will have a positive impact on your life, especially if you've done some advance planning.

Getting the Most out of "Coming Out"

Making the decision to share your secrets may be the hardest thing you've ever done. But once the decision is made, preparing yourself isn't that different from preparing for any other challenge in your life, whether it's taking a big exam, acting in a play, or going on a college or job interview.

> **To improve the odds that the rewards of sharing yourself will outweigh the risks, you should have some definite goals and a clear idea of how you plan to reach them.**

You'll have to consider the impact of the new way you'll be communicating. The nature of communication with someone who has been entrenched in an eating disorder is often one-sided or absent. So in a way, coming out is a signal that you're ready to reinstate two-way communication even though you may be out of practice. Try to imagine how you'll express your needs and expectations to others. Think about what it will feel like to have others bounce their ideas off yours and to actually consider their positions.

Ask yourself the following questions and write your answers in your journal or notebook:

- What do I hope to accomplish by coming out, both now and in the long run?

Do you really want help in overcoming the eating disorder or do you just want to get people off your case because you're sick of being the object of so much scrutiny? Do you want to take an active role in your recovery and do most of the work yourself with the least possible input from outside sources? Or are you able and willing to get a variety of people constructively involved in your life and work with them toward a common goal? Are you looking for sympathy? Do you want to rekindle old relationships that have been hurt by the eating disorder, break ties with the past, have old and new relationships blend into a different present reality for you? What *are* your short-term, intermediate, and long-term goals?

• Who do I want involved with me in this process?

Do you want to involve family and friends right away, or rely first on the help and advice of doctors, therapists, or self-help groups? Do you want a combination of people (professional and family/ friends) involved in your quest for health? When you select a friend to confide in, do you know for sure that the person can handle the responsibility of knowing about your problem? Will he or she keep it in confidence? Is there any likelihood that your confidence will be breached and other people will find out about your situation? Are you prepared for that possibility? What will you tell your friend about why you're sharing this information and what you hope will happen as a result?

If you plan to confide in family members, are you willing to accept the possibility that their reactions may not all be positive? How do you plan to react if they say things you really don't want to hear?

If you think sharing your innermost thoughts with friends and family may be more stressful than successful, but you still want to tell someone, seek out a therapist, teacher, clergyperson, school nurse, school counselor or other trusted person who will help you devise successful ways to talk to those other people. Make a list of the 10 "ideal" people you would want to talk with, starting with your first choice as number one.

- Where and when will I actually come out?

Do you envision a family gathering at which you'll make a formal declaration? Will you come out gradually, giving clues when it seems appropriate, but without a specific plan? Will you come out only if confronted and specifically asked about your eating habits or do you see yourself voluntarily telling all? Will you go to a self-help group and come out in that type of protective environment before you open up to family and friends? Will you do it anonymously by participating in an online eating disorder-oriented chat room, or contacting a resource like a hotline or helpline?

- What will I say and how will I say it?

Will you want to just discuss the facts about your eating behaviors or do you think you'll feel secure enough to discuss the emotions and motivations that support those behaviors as well? Will you be willing to delve into issues of family dynamics one-on-one with your relatives, or do you want a third party such as a therapist or counselor with you for such discussions? What tone of voice will you use? Will you allow yourself to express all your feelings, including anger?

Here are some productive and proactive opening lines to begin the coming-out process:

- *"I'm ready to discuss some things about myself that might make you uncomfortable. I need to know whether you think we can talk without your lecturing or yelling at me."*

- *"I have a problem with food and eating. I think you're probably aware of this. I don't know what to do about it and I'd like to hear your thoughts. Here's what's going on..."*

- *"I have what I think is an eating disorder. I can't handle it by myself anymore and I need some help from you. I'm not sure what kind of help, though. Can we discuss the possibilities?"*

- *"All the things that were worrying you about me are true. You were right to be concerned. I wasn't ready to hear it before, but I'm willing to talk now. I want you to know how scared I am to do this."*

- *"I don't like what's happening to me anymore. I may not like what you have to say, but I want your opinion about what I should do."*

- *"I can't guarantee how I'll react when we talk, but I'm tired of all the tension around here. I'm anorexic/bulimic/anorexic and bulimic and I need to know how you feel about that."*

If you feel you can't say things face-to-face, write a letter and ask for a written response. This technique is useful because you will have a record of each person's thoughts, which will be the foundation upon which your recovery builds.

- What will I do if I get criticized?

Can a dialogue exist when there is criticism or will you retreat and refuse to continue the discussion? Do you imagine being able to ask your critics for clarification? Will you accept that criticism might be part of the experience of coming out or will you put up your defenses? Could you express your feelings about being criticized with others who were uninvolved in this dialogue, like a therapist or close friend who can give you a safe place to vent?

Scripting the Possibilities

A wonderful way to maximize the positive effects of coming out is to write out some scripts in advance of the process. Think about what will happen when you come out—who will be involved, where and when it will be, what the dialogue will sound like, and what the end results will be. Do a "worst-case scenario" (a scene in which everything that you would *not* want to happen, does) and a "best-case scenario" (a scene in which everything works out as you'd hoped). Later, write the "actual-case scenario" after you've talked. Share them all with your family. How many of the "best-case" elements actually happened? Build on these strengths to help you recover. How many of the "worst-case" elements actually happened? Your therapist can help you address and alter or eliminate those.

Here are two scripts that might reflect your own.

Worst-Case Scenario Script

> *Participants:* Mom, Dad, Danny (8 years), Paula (12 years), me (Gabby, 16 years)
>
> *Time:* After Dad gets home from work and before dinner
>
> *Place:* The family room in our house
>
> *Me:* "I've decided to be honest about myself with all of you."
>
> *Paula:* "You couldn't be honest if your life depended on it."
>
> *Mom:* "Paula, stop it!"
>
> *Dad:* "This better be important. I have a business meeting later and I need to eat and get out of here fast."
>
> *Danny:* "What's for dinner? What's for dinner?"
>
> *Me:* "Isn't anyone listening to me?
>
> *Paula:* "Everyone listens to you, Gabby, but you always make us out to be bad guys and you make it seem like nobody ever pays attention to you. Is it about how thin you are? Do you want us to tell you how great you look?"
>
> *Mom:* "Gabby, please don't get into another argument with your sister. Just talk."

> *Me:* "What's the point? You think you know what I'm going to say even before I say it. I don't know why I thought you'd hear me now. I'm going to my room. Don't bother calling me for dinner."

Results: Things stay the same between me and the rest of the family. I'll keep on not eating because I know it gets a rise out of Paula at least. Maybe if I get real sick or something, they'll start listening to me.

Best-Case Scenario Script

(Same participants, same time and place as in above script)

> *Me:* "I've decided to be honest about myself with all of you."

> *Mom and Dad:* "We've been waiting for this for a long time."

> *Me:* "I think I'm anorexic."

> *Mom and Dad:* "We've known that for a while, but you never seem to want to talk."

> *Paula:* "And you think I'm just a silly little kid! But I'm worried about you, too. I wish I could help. I feel so sad and guilty that I can't."

> *Mom:* "What do you want us to do? We'd like to try to understand you, but we're afraid to push you too hard. You look so fragile right now."

> *Danny:* "When's dinner? I'm hungry."

> *Me:* "You're so lucky, Danny. I'm scared of eating."

> *Mom:* "Is it my cooking? Should I buy other foods for you?"

> *Me:* "No, Mom, it's not that. It's that I want to be thin. I *have* to be really thin."

Dad: "You were fine the way you used to be. You didn't have to make yourself thin. We loved you any way you were; well, we didn't like the Goth phase and I'm not thrilled that you dipped the bottom of your hair so that it's bright orange, but Mom and I will always love you. You're smart and cute and nice..."

Me: "But you never told me any of this before. You never told me I was okay; I never knew you approved of me."

Mom: "We thought you knew how we felt."

(etc.)

Results: I "hear" my family say things I never heard before. I feel they're concerned about me and that they love me, but I think they don't understand me yet. A real dialogue can happen from here. I think they're on my side.

Unanticipated Situations

When you do decide to share your secret, unanticipated situations might occur that could catch you off guard. One person might reveal something that frightens you; someone else might be so blunt that you're unprepared to hear not only *what's* being said, but also *how* it's being said. If and when that happens, it's important to admit that you're surprised or a little scared; you can then use that honesty as an opportunity to launch into a deeply felt, sincere discussion.

> **Whatever happens, though, secrecy is never an option.**

Secrecy encourages the maintenance of eating-disordered thoughts and behaviors; being open and honest helps you overcome them.

Here are some examples of such sticky situations.

Unanticipated Situation #1: Your parent doesn't seem to care that you have an eating disorder.

> *After I started vomiting on a daily basis, I became very depressed and decided to tell my mom so she could help me. When I did, she acted like it wasn't a big deal and told me not to do it anymore. It wasn't that easy. My mom knows I didn't quit throwing up but she never really says anything. It makes me feel like she doesn't care. I often feel like committing suicide and tell myself that I don't deserve to live.*
>
> *– Lucia P., age 16*

Sometimes parents don't say anything about a child's eating disorder because of fear: fear of offending you, fear of finding out the truth, fear of losing your love, fear of making things worse for you. Sometimes parents don't say anything because they literally don't know what to say. They may not understand what's happening and don't have the words to talk with you in the way you need and want. Sometimes parents don't speak out because of their own frustration and anger at not being able to stop their child's eating disorder, and they figure that keeping quiet is preferable to saying (or doing) something ugly or destructive.

When you do decide to tell your family and friends about your eating disorder, you must clarify what you need and expect from them. It may take several tries until you feel like they "get it."

However, some families can't or won't meet the needs of their loved one. They might not have the communication skills or style to do so. If that's your situation, don't blame yourself. Don't assume there was something wrong with your request. Each of us has to cope with situations in our families that are less than perfect and for which we're not directly responsible. Sometimes it's better to say, "It is what it is," rather than fight the things you can't change. There are always other people who can offer the validation that you seek—teachers, friends, their parents, counselors, or therapists.

Unanticipated Situation #2: Your parent has or had an eating disorder.

> *When I came out, my mom confessed that she has bulimia, which has its good and bad sides. We need to be there for each other for support, but it's hard because either we concentrate too much on our problem, or the other's. It's a delicate situation to live with; she's overprotective and quick-tempered, and we argue about food, appearance, and our treatment of each other.*
>
> *— Marla G., age 17*

This situation can be ticklish, but it can also lead to incredible discussions and amazing depths of understanding between parent and child. When differences occur, make a contract to "agree to disagree" about certain issues that can't be resolved immediately. Promise that neither of you will pretend, cover-up, or lie about what's going on. Admit that since you both have intimate knowledge of the physical and emotional consequences of an eating disorder, each of you will worry about the other more intensely than would otherwise be "normal" and will probably over-scrutinize one another. If you then worry that personal privacy will be elusive or impossible, talk about it.

Discuss what it was like to hear your mom admit she had an eating disorder. Tell her if it triggers a sense of competition in you. Do you feel added pressure to maintain perfect control? Are you worried that you won't be able to admit a binge-purge urge or that you had a bulimic episode? You may believe your parent has command over her eating disorder when, in fact, she doesn't. You may be concerned that if you relapse, your mom might be triggered and relapse in response.

Your mother might be just as concerned that you will be in control of your disorder and she won't be in control of hers. She may be experiencing an overwhelming sense of guilt because she believes she is somehow responsible for you becoming bulimic or anorexic. Either of you might feel annoyed at the other because people with eating disorders often like to believe they're unique, as if they've *discovered* their particular disorder. It's hard to admit that being anorexic or bulimic isn't unique; it can be even more difficult when someone in your family is engaged in the same behaviors.

To further complicate matters, you could conclude that you're a clone of your parent, someone without a separate identity. Discovering that you and your mother each struggle with an eating disorder may magnify what you don't like about her, obscure what you do like, and undermine your confidence that you will ever be able to become your own person. You need to talk about all these issues together. If that seems unsafe or too hard, find a therapist to help you do so.

Unanticipated Situation #3: You tell your boyfriend about your eating disorder and he makes fun of your problem.

> *I finally got up the nerve to admit to my boyfriend that I was anorexic and had been seeing a therapist for a month. He acted like it was a joke and told me he'd been a recovering alcoholic for ten months now—that was a REAL problem. He'd been abstinent from liquor since joining Alcoholics Anonymous right when we started dating.*
>
> *My boyfriend told me the only way to get better was to get in a self-help setup like his at AA and that I was crazy to waste my money on a shrink. He made it sound so cut and dried, like his road to recovery was better than mine. It was like we were playing "dueling therapies" or something.*
>
> *Now I have doubts about my therapy, and I'm scared that if I choose to stick with it, my boyfriend won't approve so I'll have to keep it a secret. What should I do?*
>
> – Sharmayne G., age 19

Recovering from any kind of addictive behavior is not a competition. Choosing a type of therapy, a therapist, or a self-help group is an intensely personal matter, and what works for one person might not be appropriate for somebody else. But the "dueling therapies" issue, as Sharmayne so aptly described, highlights a problem that males often have when trying to understand eating disorders. It's not just about therapy; it's about point-of-view. Men will often admit that they "just don't get it" when their daughters, wives, or girlfriends try to explain their eating-disordered behaviors and thoughts. For the most part, men in our society are brought up to think about body shape and weight differently than women, so it can be very difficult for them to empathize with the pressure to be thin that is felt by so many women.

That said, anyone who would imply that an eating disorder isn't a "real" problem needs to be set straight. Sharmayne's boyfriend (and others like him) should be challenged to read books and articles about eating disorders; at the same time, Sharmayne needs to read and learn about his problem. They can then compare and contrast one another's situations and perhaps support each other's therapies. The bottom line, though, is that the only person who has to approve of your therapy and your therapist is you.

Unanticipated Situation #4: Your parent makes you feel guilty for wanting therapy.

> *I'm relapsing into bulimia and I'm seeing a psychiatrist, but it's not enough to help me. I only spend 20 minutes with her at a time. I guess the biggest thing is my dad, and how he makes me feel guilty when I ask for more therapy. I know it's an expense but my insurance covers a lot and I've offered to pay for some of the copays. Why won't he let me get help? I have to stop this once and for all.*
>
> *– Payton G., age 20*

Unfortunately, economics often play a role in the process of finding a therapist and then being able to continue in therapy long enough to recover and sustain that recovery. Payton's experience is all too common. Also, although it appears to be an economic issue, there may be another dynamic at work here. Because she is relapsing, chances are good that her dad does not believe she is serious about another round of therapy. He may not understand that it can take several attempts before she will "get it" and make recovery a constant in her life. He may be feeling angry and frustrated and is using the cost factor to exert his power over her and her disorder. In any event, if her dad won't yield and help her pay for additional sessions, Payton can:

- ask her current psychiatrist to refer her to another therapist on her insurance plan who might be able to speak with her for longer periods of time per session (a typical therapy "hour" is between 45 and 50 minutes in length);

- see if there are groups either on or off campus to enhance her current therapy situation (Overeaters Anonymous has free groups that are open to anorexics and bulimics, and college counseling services can provide referrals);

- call local hospitals for lists of therapists who treat eating disorders and might slide their fee scales if they are not covered by the person's insurance. Internet websites pertinent to eating disorders have lists of licensed therapists.

The bottom line is that Payton needs to be proactive regardless of her dad's position.

If you have read thus far in this book, and even done some of the exercises, then it should be obvious to you (and everyone around you) that you're serious about getting control of your eating disorder. Can you envision an alternate reality, a present and a future free from the thoughts and behaviors that have dominated your life?

Ten Thing to Recognize about the Challenges of "Coming Out"

1. Even though you might want to, it's not possible (or wise) to keep your eating disorder a secret indefinitely.

2. Other people who notice your eating disorder symptoms will probably try to get you to "change" what you're doing and thinking long before you decide to "come out."

3. If you decide to "come out" on your own, you may be able to avoid feeling that a power struggle exists between you and the people who challenge your eating-disordered lifestyle.

4. It's better to "come out" than to be "found out" because when you "come out" YOU are taking charge and inviting people to help you deal with the disorder.

5. When you "come out" you demystify your situation and clarify what's going on in your daily life.

6. "Coming out" is an act of courage that shows you're strong enough to be vulnerable and flexible enough to change your thoughts and behaviors.

7. "Coming out" is a signal that you're ready to reinstate two-way communication and not let your eating disorder keep you isolated from other people.

8. You can maximize the positive effects of "coming out" by thinking about who you want to involve, when and where you want to do it, and what you will say.

9. Write out scripts to anticipate what might happen when you "come out."

10. Be prepared for unanticipated glitches, but don't second-guess your decision to "come out" and don't waver in your resolve.

chapter eight

What to Expect in Therapy

"I was dieting for over a year, and on the verge of being really sick. The more I dieted, the more I needed to diet. I kept saying I was losing weight because I wanted to. But actually, the restricting was like a demon pushing from inside me . . .and in all the wrong directions. I guess I was lucky. I met a girl at school who'd done the same thing and she helped me realize I couldn't kick it myself. She'd been there and encouraged me to go to therapy. She was like my guide out of a maze."

— Penny L., age 16

Having an eating disorder *is* like entering a maze without map or compass, uncertain where the exits are or how you'll find them. What's more, an extended struggle with an eating disorder can make you so emotionally and physically exhausted that you don't have enough energy to even *look* for a way out.

To complicate your dilemma, people outside that metaphorical maze are an added source of confusion. You can't understand why those who profess to love and care about you do and say things that feel neither loving nor caring. You may hear comments that your behavior is "wrong," "dangerous," "crazy," "illogical," "abnormal," "disgusting," "stupid," "incomprehensible." The words hurt and feel like insults or barbs that lodge deep within your emotional core. So you protect yourself by retreating further into the maze of your disorder.

Meanwhile, these same loved-ones are equally frustrated and angry. Not only are they nervous about your physical and emotional status and fearful you could die, but they can't get you to change. What you're doing scares them and they want it to stop. Maybe you do too.

Perhaps you've tried to overcome your eating disorder on your own, but nothing has worked. You may have relapsed so often that you now assume it will always be the dominant force in your life. This exhausted, depressed resignation is sometimes called "hitting a wall" or "bottoming out." It is a low point that feels so awful that you are willing to see the value of getting some support beyond your immediate friendships and family. You realize that you don't have to be isolated and alone with your illness or in your recovery and that you can ask for and get professional help.

These professional helpers are typically "therapists" who can be objective about you and your situation because they're not emotionally involved the way family members or friends would be. They work *with* you and *for* you.

> **Your agreement to accept help from a therapist
> is a sign of strength and courage.**

The stubbornness that has kept you "stuck" in your eating disorder for so long can now be turned into an asset. It will help you stick to your recovery whenever ambivalence makes you wonder what you've gotten yourself into.

Therapy Is a Partnership

Some people believe that "going into therapy" means that a psychiatrist will decide and dictate what they should think and how they should act. In fact, psychiatrists are not the only kind of professionals who can help you, and, therapy isn't like that at all.

Therapy is a two-way street, a partnership between you and your helper(s), of whom there are many different kinds (described later in this chapter). Not only will your therapist listen to you and make suggestions about how you can improve your life, but you will listen to the therapist and discuss those suggestions. Ultimately, *together* you come to an accurate understanding of your situation and what's best for you. Although this can be uncomfortable, especially if what the therapist has to say isn't what you want to hear, it gives you the opportunity and the tools to grow and change in a positive direction.

Therapy is a cooperative venture that develops its own particular characteristics and tempo over a period of time. It's somewhat like a relationship between coach and athlete. A therapist and coach do similar things: give you the "rules of the game," teach you strategies for dealing with an opponent, motivate, show you ways to practice and hone your skills, help you deal with victory as well as defeat, and prepare you to eventually "go it alone."

An athlete and someone in therapy also have similar missions: to listen to the suggestions of the person teaching them, learn the skills behind those suggestions; internalize that skill base; then practice, practice, practice until the skills become second-nature. Then they are a part of your "muscle memory," only in this case the "muscle" refers to your thought patterns and behaviors.

> **Therapy offers a structured setting in which you can safely and comfortably allow yourself to grow and change in productive, non-eating-disordered ways.**

It is crucial that a foundation of trust exist between the partners in therapy, because an honest exchange of information is then possible. Trust evolves gradually over time as people get to know one another. *You must be open and honest with your therapist if you feel as though trust is lacking at any stage. Without it, you can't work through the intense emotions and tough discussions that inevitably occur, and you're apt to distort a therapist's responses and reactions to you.* (In Chapter 12, "Sustaining Recovery," you'll find a discussion about these "cognitive distortions" and you'll learn how to catch yourself when you're in that mode of thinking.)

Therapy can also be fun, uplifting and fascinating. In fact, the process is a lot like writing: it comes in fits and starts with bursts of inspiration and occasional lapses into writer's block. Sometimes it's just a matter of starting the work and waiting for the "Aha's!" when pieces fall into place.

Therapists' Styles

Just as there are coaches with different styles for motivating their athletes, therapists, too, can have different styles. Although all therapists are catalysts for change, some give you a lot of responsibility for your own recovery and want you to rely more on yourself than on them. Others are less democratic and take a more directive approach by expecting you to depend upon them to give you the answers. In general, most therapists are flexible, with styles that vary from week to week.

You may find that some therapists will acknowledge that they're working for you, that you've hired them and technically you can fire them. This is meant to remind you that you have a great deal of power in this relationship. Many will also tell you that the work they do for you depends on your participation in the process. They have the questions but *you* have the answers. They see patterns that you can't yet see, will help you focus so that you *can*, and teach you the skills necessary to continue the process.

Some therapists are comfortable with "self-disclosure" and are willing to talk a bit about themselves during a session, if doing so is appropriate to the ongoing therapy. In fact, many people who work in the field of eating disorders have recovered from the disorders themselves and will share their experiences during therapy. Others refuse to divulge any personal information, either because of their training or personal preference.

> **Whatever the person's style, there needs to be a good fit and comfortable chemistry between the two of you.**

Your Treatment Team

The usual mix of professionals who will help you through the various phases of eating disorder recovery are typically referred to as your "treatment team." They include:

- a *medical doctor* (M.D.) such as a pediatrician or internist who does your physical exam (including blood work, urine checks, bone density checks, and weekly weigh-ins if indicated), and who can prescribe medication as needed to assist your recovery;

- a *psychiatrist* (also an M.D.) who talks with you about your thoughts and feelings, evaluates you for the presence of coexisting (comorbid) conditions, and also prescribes mood-altering medication and adjusts it as needed;

- a *licensed clinical social worker* or *psychologist* (often the primary "talking therapist"), who may also coordinate the therapy you're receiving from the other team members;

- a *nutritionist* or *licensed dietitian* who evaluates your food intake and creates a food plan, adjusting it as you progress in recovery.

Less typical but also desirable is a team that includes the "expressive" therapies of art and movement, so you may work with:

- an *art therapist* who helps you literally "draw out" your emotions;

- a *movement therapist* who helps you become comfortable in your body as you redefine what it means to literally "take up space."

The members of your team collaborate and periodically speak with one another, an approach that keeps you accountable to recovery, catches you if you are blatantly dishonest with any of them, and thwarts major setbacks.

The Intake Interviews: The General Intake

No matter where you go for therapy, the first meeting with a therapist or team of therapists is called an *intake*. It may involve only you, you together with your family, or you alone followed by a separate interview with your family. The professional you first encounter might be your "talking therapist" or it might be someone else who does the intake and then gives the results to the person who will become your therapist. In either case, you will be asked many detailed questions designed to elicit a lot of information in a short period of time. You might also have to fill out one or more written questionnaires.

Even if the initial intake experience seems overwhelming, alarming, or intrusive, give it your best. If you don't, and you're not honest and direct, the interviewer might make an incorrect initial diagnosis. He or she might even think your problem isn't really an eating disorder and suggest that you should focus your therapy efforts on something else. If you misrepresent yourself on intake, or worse, are hostile, the interviewer/therapist could think you're not really ready for therapy, and recommend that you wait until you *are* ready or that you go elsewhere for treatment (though this doesn't usually happen).

Although no two intakes are exactly alike, all ask for basic information: name, social security number, address and phone number, date of birth, school or occupation, and names of the people with whom you live. You will also be asked about your previous medical history: the names of prior doctors or therapists, if you are currently taking any medication (what kinds, what dosages), if you've ever been hospitalized, and if you have, why? You can expect questions about your menstrual cycle (if you're female), sexual history, use or abuse of tobacco, drugs, laxatives, diet pills, or alcohol, and physically self-injurious thoughts and behaviors.

The intake interviewer will want to know about your parents or guardians: their names and addresses, marital status, and any mental or physical health problems (past and present) of your immediate or extended family. Even if you don't have all the answers, try to give as much accurate information as you can.

The questions pertaining to the eating disorder will vary, and may seem to you the most unsettling of all. Here are some more possible topics:

diets and dieting history

physical symptoms since the onset of your eating issues

binge behaviors

purge episodes

preferred methods of purging

restrictive/anorexic behaviors

traumatic or transitional events in your life

Individual Therapy

Individual therapies all involve a one-on-one relationship with a therapist. An example is *psychoanalysis*, which focuses intensely on your past as a means to understand what's happening to you now. Some are *long-term*, which means you can expect to meet at least once a week for a year or more. *Short-term therapy* is designed to last less than a year, often less than six months.

Behavioral therapy teaches you how to change your behaviors but doesn't require that you do a lot of self-analysis about why those behaviors came to play a part in your life. It looks at the stimulus-response patterns that support certain behavior chains, and then gives you the tools to change those behaviors, slowly, as if you were working one link of a chain at a time.

Think about how you would teach a puppy to sit. You can't just say "Sit!" and expect it to do what you ask. You teach it through a series of steps, correcting and rewarding each success along the way, and knowing in advance that it will take time. People aren't so different from puppies insofar as we respond to clear messages and rewards and are often successful when complicated behaviors are broken down into manageable units. We also need permission to practice, make mistakes, and try again.

Cognitive therapy (CT) focuses on your thoughts and how your beliefs and perceptions shape your emotional responses. This type of therapy teaches you to recognize the unproductive and disapproving ways in which you think and talk about yourself, sometimes called "scripts," "themes in your thinking," or "negative self-talk." Once you're aware of these negative patterns, you can understand how they contributed to the development and maintenance of your eating disorder and you can challenge and change them.

Cognitive-behavioral therapy (CBT) blends cognitive and behavioral strategies in a limited time frame to achieve specific goals that you and your therapist agree on at the outset of therapy. CBT is a structured treatment: some therapists use manuals to guide what you will do each week, much like a teacher with a course outline. Usually, you'll get homework assignments designed to augment whatever you've accomplished in your one-on-one sessions and speed your progress when you're away from the therapist's office.

CBT can sometimes be mislabeled as "too simple." It isn't. CBT is focused and detail-oriented, helps you set and reach goals, and gives you strategies to evaluate how far you've come on your recovery path. It also encourages you to acknowledge positive changes as they occur, integrate them into your daily behaviors, and use them as building blocks for the next phase of treatment.

CT and CBT are known to foster positive change relatively quickly. Since therapist's fees and insurance reimbursements can be major concerns, and since managed care rarely approves more than 30 therapy sessions per year, these strategies are favored by health-care insurers.

Family Therapy

Family therapy is a crucial component of the healing process because eating disorders are often a response to problems within the family, such as difficulties with open expression of feelings, conflict, and lack of support between family members. An eating disorder can also be a response to familial trauma such as addictions, mental illness, sexual, physical or emotional abuse, suicide attempts or suicides, incarceration, or any other major stressor.

With the guidance of the therapist, family members can learn to work together for constructive change. In family sessions, you might discover how to:

- pinpoint triggers that escalate your disorder, discuss their impact on you, and learn how others in your family react to the same triggers;

- identify your communication styles;

- use "I language" when talking with one another ("I feel frustrated," "I need support," "I'm proud of you");

- recognize and avoid using "You" language ("You make me feel guilty," "You make me so angry!"), which can sound accusatory and creates tension, blame, and a tendency for the other person to deny the truth of your statement;

- modify "You" statements and turn them into clearer "I" statements;

- be respectful of one another's viewpoints;

- acknowledge and manage feelings effectively, especially anger;
- be realistic about setting goals and achieving them.

As hard as it is to admit you're anorexic or bulimic, it can be even harder to own up to the probability that something in the way your family operates has played a part in your eating issues. You might feel protective or even responsible for maintaining family harmony and happiness. But that responsibility is *never* solely yours, and family therapy can be a safe place to talk about this kind of delicate issue. Together, you can try to identify, discuss, and repair many of the delicate, sensitive issues that maintain your eating disorder.

Therapist-Led Group Therapy

Group therapy involves meeting with several unrelated people who have similar problems. "Therapist-led" group therapy means exactly that—it is led by a professional, and usually takes place in a therapist's office. There are a variety of group formats, depending on your stage of recovery and the availability of groups. A *time-limited group* runs for a specific number of sessions. Since every member enters and leaves at the same time, a group "culture" develops quickly, and members tend to develop skills at a similar pace. *Open-ended* groups run continuously throughout the year and allow people to enter and leave when they are ready to. Therefore, members may be at dissimilar stages of recovery with different skill levels. Some groups have a specific focus, such as a "mother's group" or an "adolescent group" or a "family group" in which members of your family join the group with you and other members' families.

It can be scary to join a group:

It was the most humiliating thing in my life when I walked into the first group session and saw five people from my school. I knew then that my secret was out and that I'd really have to

face up to my anorexia. I thought it'd be blabbed all over
school the next day: "Ann's in therapy. Ann's got an eating
disorder." As if everyone didn't already know.

– Ann B., age 15

Ann "freaked out" unnecessarily. Groups operate according to two principles that prevent humiliation and "blabbing." First, participants must pledge to maintain *confidentiality*. That means nobody will reveal what is said inside the group to anyone outside the group unless specific permission is given to do so. Additionally, members must agree that any criticism of a group member will be *constructive*. If those conditions are missing from a group in which you participate, find another group.

In the majority of cases, however, participation in a group will help you come out of isolation and enhance your perspective about problems and solutions. It will also enable you to risk emotional self-disclosure to "strangers" who become "confidantes," and who learn how to support one other during (and sometimes after) recovery.

Nutrition Therapy

Nutrition therapy takes place in both individual and group formats and involves frequent consultations with a *licensed dietitian* or *nutritionist*. (I will use the terms interchangeably, although a "dietitian" is licensed, whereas a "nutritionist" may not be.) This helper will determine if you have an adequate, accurate understanding of the role of food and nutrition in your life, will challenge and correct your misinformation, and help you devise meal plans and eating strategies to combat your disordered thinking and behaving.

Nutritionists are hard to con or fool. Much as the "talking therapist" perceives themes and patterns in your thinking, or an art therapist is alert to colors and shapes in your drawings, a nutritionist attends to patterns that have to do with food and eating. Your weight, muscle tone, or body-fat percentage, and the entries you write down in your food diaries will support or challenge your verbal "stories." You may resist talking about these issues, or feel ashamed or exposed if forced to do so, but many of you assert that dietitians are your most valuable resource and that therapy wouldn't work as well without them.

Expressive Therapies: Art and Movement

Art and movement therapies are considered "expressive" because they help you explore how and why you use your body to communicate inner issues. Expressive techniques are also excellent tools to break through barriers to physical self-acceptance and help overcome body image distortion and body hatred.

Art therapy projects are "hands on" and involve the world of your imagination. You may find yourself making a "body map," filling in an outline of a body with paints, markers, crayons, drawing shapes, writing "feeling" words inside that outline. Or you may be asked to imagine a container into which you'll place the negative "stuff" that makes you uncomfortable in your body and contributes to your negative body image. You then make the actual container and its contents. Perhaps you'll create a photo album with images of you at various stages of your life, including a time in the future.

What often happens with these kinds of therapies is that feelings and beliefs that are difficult to verbalize become more clear by taking artistic form. Also, your art therapist can point out any symbols and patterns in your work as well as how integrated the images become as you heal. You can choose to discuss whatever emerges during the art therapy sessions or during your individual or group therapy sessions.

Movement therapy releases feelings in your body. Although most of us label something as a "feeling" when it pops up in our heads, movement therapists teach you to focus on the literal *feelings* that exist *in the body*. Since people with eating disorders are usually afraid of sensations felt in the body, movement therapists can help you overcome those fears. You learn to locate the emotions in your body, express them through movement, take the risk to become visible, and feel safe when you are.

Inpatient vs Outpatient Therapies

Therapy can take place in a number of settings depending on the severity of your disorder. If you are physically ill and your habit pattern is uncontrollable when you begin treatment, you may choose to (or your therapist may recommend that you) enter a hospital. You will then be an *inpatient* on a medical floor (depending upon your age, this will most likely be either pediatrics or internal medicine) or on a unit with psychiatric patients (most often people recovering from drug or alcohol dependencies and a variety of mental disturbances).

Some hospitals set aside a certain number of "beds" and call the special section an "eating disorder unit," which is usually staffed by doctors, nurses, and other therapists who are specially trained to help you understand and confront your particular challenges. Since patients in these units have similar problems, intense bonds of shared experiences develop and therapy often progresses relatively quickly.

Sometimes a person is so ill and in so much denial about the seriousness of the situation, that parents or legal guardians may decide to "involuntarily" admit their loved one to the hospital. This is a controversial step both legally and ethically. However, a study conducted by researchers at the University of Iowa School of Medicine found that even the patients who expressed negative attitudes toward certain parts of the hospitalization appreciated the help they received and did improve clinically over the short-term. (Watson, et al., "Involuntary Treatment of Patients with Eating Disorders," *Eating Disorders Review,* March/April, 2001).

Alternatives to inpatient hospitalization are *day treatment programs* (similar to the experience of going to school all day long), or *intensive outpatient programs* (can be daytime or evening, meets less often than daily, runs fewer hours per day), where you go home at night. These programs, usually affiliated with a hospital or specialized eating disorder facility, are often considered "step-downs" from the more intense hospital experience. They provide help with the transition from 24/7 therapeutic support to "real life" and are frequently covered by insurance plans.

Drug Therapy

When you meet with a psychiatrist during your initial therapy sessions, it's possible that you'll be offered medication as part of your treatment. Drug therapy for eating disorders began many years ago when doctors discovered that some medicines originally used to treat other diseases helped alleviate some of the more obvious symptoms of anorexia and bulimia. These drugs also had a beneficial effect on the anxiety, panic, compulsions, and obsessions that are characteristic of eating-disordered thinking and behaving. Several drugs are used today, and new ones are added when the FDA deems them safe. Consequently, doctors are continuously updating their knowledge about how these medications can maximize symptom relief with a minimum of uncomfortable side effects.

The basic categories of these medications are:

• *Tricyclic antidepressants* — invented in the 1960s, formerly used to treat depression, but found to have serious side effects. Today, they have been largely replaced by serotonin reuptake inhibitors.

• *Monoamine Oxidase (MAO) Inhibitors* — another class of antidepressants that combat serious depression but can have life-threatening side effects if taken in combination with other drugs or certain foods.

• *Selective Serotonin Reuptake Inhibitors (SSRIs)* — the first-line antidepressants of choice, often effective, with few side effects. However, weight gain can be a side effect (especially with Prozac and Paxil). Many combine the antidepressant action with anxiety-reducing, sedative components.

Medication Compliance

The decision to take any medication must be an "informed" one, meaning that you understand the benefits and the risks of your choice and agree to be "medication (med) compliant." In practice, this means you will follow the doctor's directions about how and when to take the drug (or combination of drugs). You won't skip any doses or stop taking the medication until you and your doctor decide they're no longer necessary or decide to change the regimen.

It's okay to be anxious about taking medicine, but it's *not* okay to turn the issue into a power struggle between you and the people who want you to recover from your eating disorder. Taking meds should not become a matter of "what they want me to do" versus "what I want to do."

Realistically, however, glitches in compliance happen all the time. Perhaps you have every intention of taking the meds but tend to "forget." Maybe you discover that you don't like the side effects or worry about being labeled "crazy." If someone questions your decision to take the medicine, you might begin to doubt it yourself and get lazy about taking them. Sometimes you'll forget to take a pill at the designated time because you're too busy, or you're embarrassed to have to go to the nurse's office where your medication is kept during the school day. Unfortunately, when you don't take the medicine in a compliant, appropriate way, you may end up with more physical problems and emotional ups and downs than if you'd never started the meds at all.

Be Informed About Your Medications

One way to get the full benefit of drug therapy is to anticipate these glitches and address your fears about taking medication. *Ask a lot of questions during the initial sessions with your psychiatrist.* For instance:

- What is the prescription for? Is it to deal with depression? Panic? Obsessions and compulsions? Anxiety? Hyperactivity?

- If this medication is an antidepressant, what kind?

- What are the possible side effects?

- Is this drug addictive? How would I know if I was becoming addicted to it?

- How long will I have to take it before I feel any relief from my symptoms? How long will I have to take it, period?

- Will it affect my appetite?

- Will it affect my weight?

- Will it make me feel noticeably different from how I am feeling now?

- Will my eating-disordered thoughts ease up? What if it makes those thoughts more intense? What if I miss having them?

- If I have a bulimic episode and vomit, will enough of the drug still be in my system to help me?

- What should I do if I miss a dose? Two doses?

- What could happen if I decided to stop taking it all at once?

- What would happen if I had a hard time taking the medicine on a consistent basis?

- What would happen if I didn't intend to take the medication but said I was going to?

Drug treatment has two phases: an "acute" phase of trial and error to figure out the most effective and tolerable dosage, and the "maintenance" phase which is a continuation of the regimen to prevent relapse. Try to be open-minded as you and your doctor work together to find the right medicine or combination of medicines to alleviate your particular symptoms. Initially, the process may be as much "art" as it is "science." Your doctor may have to "tweak" your medications several times until the right balance is achieved.

The side effects for most drugs will be minimal, tolerable, and temporary. Since it's impossible to predict with 100% accuracy what these effects will be, your doctor can alter the dosage or change the drug regimen if they're making you feel too uncomfortable. In any case, *you shouldn't feel worse after taking a drug than before you began taking it.*

Depending on the symptom(s) targeted by the drug(s), you can expect some physical and mental changes. These might include a sense of a burden being lifted, an optimism that had been missing, an absence of fear, or the sense that empty holes within you have been filled with positive emotions and thoughts. On one hand, you may find more energy to do things, and on the other, you may be more relaxed, able to sleep through the nights without disturbing dreams or periods of wakefulness. Now, you may want to sleep, not to escape sadness and depression, but because you're simply tired. Your appetite may improve, you might enjoy a renewed sense of taste and smell, and the compulsion to binge and purge may be less appealing, compelling, and less logical.

Some changes will happen within a matter of days; others will take longer because the "therapeutic" level of a drug (the amount it takes to *really* make a difference) builds up in your bloodstream over time. Many people feel an immediate rush of optimism about recovery when meds are added to their therapy regimen because medications are a "concrete" and specific way to help the process.

Therapy Unfolds

If you have anorexia and/or bulimia and decide to go into therapy, you may be exposed to all these therapy formats at one time or another. Many people may be involved in your care at the same time, but that just makes the process interesting and helps you learn to express yourself effectively and accurately. The process may sound more complicated than it really is. Therapy unfolds; it won't bowl you over. You won't be faced with everything at once. Therapy isn't designed to frighten or overwhelm you, though at times it may seem overwhelming and scary. It's an opportunity to be challenged, learn to set goals, establish priorities, test strategies, succeed, goof up, succeed again, and eventually find your way out of the eating disorder maze.

Ten Things to Remember about What to Expect in Therapy

1. Therapy is a cooperative venture to help you understand your situation and gain skills necessary for recovery.

2. Therapy occurs in a variety of settings depending on the severity of your illness: in-patient, non-residential day treatment, intensive outpatient, and weekly outpatient.

3. Many different kinds of therapists will work with you throughout your recovery. A typical treatment team includes medical doctors, psychologists, social workers, dietitians (nutritionists), art and movement therapists.

4. There are many different styles of therapy, and you have the right to ask your therapist to explain their approach.

5. There are a variety of therapy formats, such as individual, family, and group.

6. Therapy offers a structured setting in which you can safely and comfortably let yourself grow and change in productive, non-eating-disordered ways.

7. The first session is usually an intake interview, when you'll be asked to provide information about yourself, your family, and the history of your eating disorder.

8. Therapy isn't designed to frighten or overwhelm you, although at times it may seem so.

9. To be most effective, therapy requires a foundation of trust between you and your helpers.

10. Therapy is a process that unfolds: you won't be faced with everything at once and it won't bowl you over.

chapter nine

Choosing a Therapist

"I'm scared to change. I'm afraid I'll fail. I'm afraid I'll succeed."
— Terry L., age 18

hanging something that's familiar to you, even if that "something" is harmful, can be difficult to do. When that "something" is an eating disorder, the motivation to change can be further complicated by your history, especially if you've previously tried and failed to overcome your problem or have spent a lot of time denying that the problem even existed. You may have little hope that you'll succeed *this* time and assume that you'll always be "stuck" in your current patterns. You might be skeptical about therapy and therapists. It's only logical, then, that you'd hesitate to ask for, much less accept, assistance.

Instead, if you've been through this before, try to "reframe" your present situation in positive, proactive terms. Whether you're having a temporary lapse in recovery or a more severe, prolonged relapse, think of the flare-up as a wake-up call that you need additional help to renew your commitment to life without an eating disorder.

If you're starting this process of recovery for the first time, your initial challenge may be to admit that *your problem won't go away by denying it exists.* In fact, the opposite usually happens: the added strains of secrecy and lying make the situation worse. What *will* make it go away is your willingness to face up to reality and to work hard on your recovery.

In either case, it takes a lot of courage to decide to face up to an adversary as tough as an eating disorder and then let a group of virtual strangers help you redirect your efforts and energies toward recovery. But you *can* do it.

How to Find the Help You Need and Want

Once you decide you're willing to try therapy, the next step is to find the right kind of help. If you're a teenager or young adult, your parents or guardians will help you do this. They've probably made most decisions about your health care, to date, and it's possible you've never before had a voice in this process. But this is one time where your input is both desirable and important. How do you begin? What are your options?

1. Find a qualified therapist who has special training in working with anorexics and bulimics.

The Academy for Eating Disorders (AED) (703/556-9222; *www.aedweb.org)* and the *International Association for Eating Disorder Professionals* (IAEDP) (877/540-5691; *www.iaedp.com*) maintain memberships lists of qualified therapists. Both of these organizations have stringent requirements for professional training before they will allow health care professionals to become members. (This doesn't mean the therapists who aren't members of either group are untrained or unprofessional. It may just mean that they have not applied for membership or haven't yet fulfilled all the continuing education and training requirements for membership.) The AED also publishes an annual directory of health care professionals with information about each member's practice (the geographic location of the office, if they work with children and adolescents or adults, if they do individual, family, or group therapy, how to make contact by phone, fax, or email). A number of other directories also exist online at websites such as the *Eating Disorders Referral Center (www.edreferral.com), Something Fishy (www.something-fishy.org)* and *Pale Reflections (www.pale-reflections.com)*. In addition, most hospitals with inpatient eating disorder units as well as other independent eating disorder treatment facilities list their staff members as part of their website information.

2. Shop around.

Since finding the right therapist is such an important part of recovery, call and/or interview as many people or places as you need or want to before making your decision. This is a common practice which is expected by most therapists. A family member might help you do the ground-work, but the more *you're* involved in this process, the greater will be your commitment to therapy.

In a way, this is similar to beginning a class in school that you're initially hesitant about. Maybe you're afraid you'll be bored or worried it will be too hard. If you sit in the back of the room, never answer questions, rarely participate in discussions, then those negative expectations will probably come true. But if you sit up front, raise your hand a lot, and get involved in activities, you might like the class so much that you *want* to come back to the next session.

3. Make a "shopping list" of the qualities of the professional "helper" or "helpers" with whom you see yourself succeeding.

Answer the following questions:

- Does the gender of the doctor or therapist matter to you? Why?

If you are a girl, would you prefer a female practitioner? If you are a boy, would you prefer a male doctor or therapist? What are the reasons for your preference? Have you had a particularly good or bad experience with a same-sex or opposite-sex health care provider in the past that has caused you to feel this way?

- Would the age of the doctor or therapist alter your willingness to work with this person? Why?

For instance, could you discuss your problems more openly with a young therapist because you'd feel more in sync? Do you think you'd have more confidence in someone older who had more professional experience? Is your reasoning based on actual past experiences with older versus younger teachers or doctors? Is your reasoning based on gut feeling?

- Does the therapist's style of working with patients matter to you?

Do you feel so overwhelmed at this moment that you think you'd prefer a directive, authoritative therapist with a clear-cut approach? Or would you like someone with a more flexible approach? Are you looking for someone who is willing to give you all the time you need to tell your story and explore your problems? Or do you want to work with someone who will dive right in and try to get things resolved quickly?

- Would you be willing to be seen by a health care provider who had worked with and was recommended by one of your friends or relatives, or would you prefer going to someone unknown by anyone else in your network of relationships? Why?

Some people find that knowing about a therapist's personality and reputation from the firsthand experience of a friend or relative eases the tension of initial visits and makes the thought of therapy a bit less unnerving. What qualities match the items on your own "therapist shopping list"? On the other hand, you might be concerned about privacy and confidentiality, and feel threatened by the thought that someone else who knows you also knows your therapist. Perhaps you're concerned that you won't be able to speak openly and honestly with a therapist who has a connection to your family or peers.

- Is there a chance that the location of the office might affect your willingness to work with the doctor or therapist?

As odd as this question might seem, many people are put off by the location of some offices. This is often the case when appointments take place in hospital-based offices, because some people find hospitals to be intimidating. Perhaps the location is hard to get to: maybe it isn't within walking distance from home, school, a bus or subway stop, or is so far from home that driving there and back takes a long time. Lots of people get sloppy about keeping appointments if getting to them is such an effort that the payoffs don't seem to outweigh the inconvenience involved. Think about this ahead of time so that the office's location won't turn into your excuse to avoid or stop therapy after you've begun.

4. Make a list of anything you would want to ask a therapist.

Here are some questions I'm frequently asked by prospective clients.

- What is your educational background?
- How long have you been a therapist?
- How and why did you become an eating disorder therapist?
- Do you or did you have an eating disorder?
- Are you a licensed professional?
- What is your preferred treatment approach?
- How much does a session cost? Do you accept insurance? Do you have a sliding fee scale if I don't have insurance that will cover your services?

- Do you prescribe medications? How do you decide what medications to prescribe?

- Will you work with me alone and have my family work with another therapist, or will we all work with the same therapist or therapy team?

- Do you offer group therapy?

- How often would we meet? How do you decide how many times we will meet?

- Can I contact you between our scheduled sessions if I need to? Will those interactions be confidential?

- Can I communicate with you by email? Will those emails be confidential?

- What will you do if I disagree with your suggestions during therapy?

- How long will it take me to know you're the right therapist for me?

- What if you and I don't click? Can you refer me to someone else? Will you be angry with me?

- Can I be forced into treatment against my will?

Any concern you have is valid; it's better to ask too many questions than too few.

When Negotiation Isn't an Option

The last question in the above list, "Can I be forced into treatment against my will?" is a very common fear of people who struggle with eating disorders. The answer to it is "Yes," *if* your eating disorder is so far advanced that your life is currently in danger.

> **In such a case, your preferences may have to be overridden by the choices that others must make, on your behalf and in your best interest, to save your life.**

You won't have a chance, then, to negotiate and choose a particular style of therapist or treatment situation. You may find yourself in an emergency room at a hospital, or on one of the inpatient facilities discussed in Chapter 8. Until your health has stabilized to a point at which life or death is not the overwhelming and overriding concern, don't expect to negotiate about anything, much less your ideal therapy situation.

How to Improve the Odds for Success

Once you've thought about the therapy environment in which you see yourself succeeding, and the style of therapist you'd like to spend such intense moments with, you may be more ready to talk about this with your parents, guardian, or any other appropriate person. Comparing your preferences with those of your family members should result in a win-win situation for everybody, even if it involves some compromise between what you want and what your family thinks you need. Whatever therapy situation you eventually end up in, give yourself credit for being actively involved in the selection process, approaching things logically, stating your needs and wants, and accepting the challenges of recovery.

> **Whomever you choose to work with, you must be honest and accurately represent your problem.**

It's especially crucial that you tell them about any and all physical problems along with the emotional issues that are bothering you. For example, if your parotid glands are swollen because you've been vomiting, admit it and don't pretend you've just had a bout of the flu. If your menstrual periods have stopped, don't say that they're irregular. If your gums and teeth are affected by bulimic vomiting, don't blame the problems on too much candy as a child, or poor heredity.

No therapist is a mind reader. If you don't speak candidly, he/ she might not ask you about the issues or situations that you feel are problematic and important to discuss. Worse, the therapist may diagnose and want to treat you first for something *other than* an eating disorder because you've been dishonest about your signs, symptoms, concerns, etc.

A New Base of Competence

By doing all this thinking and preplanning, you've effectively changed the focus of your life from problems to solutions, from negatives to positives. You've made a commitment to therapy and taken the first steps. You're now at a potential transition point in your relationship with family and friends; you've confronted yourself and your eating disorder; you've admitted the need for help and taken the steps to find it; you've shown your strength and guts, and your willingness to grow. You've proven that you can be assertive and self-aware; your words and actions show that you can be capable, rational, and assume *appropriate* control of some aspects of your life. You are building a foundation of competence—success breeds success, and confidence comes with competence.

Competence is a powerful word that implies readiness, skill, ability, fitness, and proficiency. From this stage of recovery on, others will continue to believe in and respect your competence as long as you remain well-informed and honest about the changes that are happening in your life. Familiarizing yourself with the clinical definitions of anorexia and bulimia that you will find in the Appendix of this book might make it easier for you to discuss your symptoms with your therapist. Take your responses to the EAT-26 (in Chapter 4 on anorexia) or your answers to the statements about bulimic behaviors (in Chapter 5 on bulimia) with you to your initial therapy sessions. Also, bring your written responses to any of the exercises throughout this book. The more concrete, current data you share about yourself, the more raw material your therapist will have to work with.

Ten Things to Remember About Finding a Therapist

1. Your input in finding a therapist is a desirable and important element in the selection process.

2. If possible, find a therapist who has special training in eating disorders.

3. List what you think would make your therapy experience successful, including characteristics of the type of place and kind of person you imagine helping you.

4. Take the time to compare and contrast your preferences with those of your parents or guardian, and see what kinds of compromises can be reached so you all feel confident.

5. Write out a list of questions you want a therapist to answer to help you and your parents decide.

6. It's okay to talk with several therapists before making the final decision about whom you will hire to work with you.

7. If your health is in grave danger, your choices and preferences may have to be overridden by immediate choices others must make to save your life.

8. No therapist is a mind reader. Once you make the commitment to therapy, it's crucial that you're honest and describe your physical and emotional issues with as much accuracy as possible.

9. Choosing a therapist is an unmistakable signal to family and friends that you have the courage, strength, and willingness to challenge and change your eating-disordered ways.

10. Your willingness to learn and share about your self and your disorder with your therapist will greatly increase your feelings of competence and confidence.

chapter ten

Working with a Nutritionist

"My nutritionist said that consistency is key. I have to be consistent with my food intake in order for my brain to let up on the obsessive thoughts about food, hunger, weight, and then I'll be able to concentrate on other things."

– Kay S., age 16

Nutrition therapy is an important component of a comprehensive treatment plan. This is because your dietitian/nutritionist will help you with any food-related issues that need to be addressed in your recovery, such as meal planning, changing habitual eating patterns, and learning the facts about calories, metabolism and the body.

Initial Session

The first visit, or "intake," with a nutritionist usually takes place within a week or so of your therapy intake interview. Although it won't necessarily "make or break" your initial forays into recovery, the process will go more smoothly *if* you let yourself trust that what the dietitian suggests is appropriate for your situation.

One of the main goals of this initial session is to create a food plan to meet your current needs—revisions will occur in an incremental fashion over time as you recover. Eventually, you will learn to "decouple," which means to separate your food and weight-related behaviors from your associated feelings and psychological issues.

The kinds of questions you'll be asked will obviously focus on your eating patterns, food preferences, allergies and feared foods, and beliefs about how certain foods impact your physical self. Expect to talk about your weight history, how you feel about your weight and your body, as well as any dieting, bingeing, restricting, or purging behaviors, including exercise habits. You'll also be discussing any tobacco, drug or alcohol use/abuse, your sexual history, and physical and psychiatric histories, noting prior or current hospitalizations, medications, or therapies, and any medical symptoms you may have, such as dizziness, weakness, cold sensitivity or bowel problems.

As you can see, the dietitian and the intake therapist solicit much of the same information. You may think it's overkill and wonder why you have to repeat yourself. However, a dietitian will listen to you with a slightly different "ear" by focusing on issues and patterns that the other therapists also address, but from a different angle.

Also, a session with a nutritionist may "feel" more like a lesson in school than a therapy session because you are learning so much new, specialized information. You will probably walk out of it with a specific food plan to try (usually based on the American Dietetic Association's food group "exchange" system) as well as a homework assignment to track your food intake, hunger and satiety (satisfaction), and emotional reactions to eating.

Nutrition 101: What You Might Learn in Initial Sessions

When you work with a dietitian or nutritionist to overcome your eating disorder, you can expect to learn a great deal about the impact of *both* adequate and inadequate nutrition on your body. You'll also learn to replace your inaccurate beliefs with the correct facts and strategies to help you recover. The first few sessions will probably address the following questions:

1. What is a calorie and what are my caloric needs?

A "calorie" is a measurement of the energy released when your body breaks down food, including carbohydrates, proteins, and fats. *Your body needs a certain number of calories in order to survive and thrive.* The more calories in a food, the more energy that food can give to your body. Under normal circumstances, if you eat more calories than you need for daily activities, your body stores the extra calories as fat and you'll gain weight; if you eat fewer calories than your body needs, you'll lose weight.

Males and females have slightly different caloric needs at different times of their lives.

> **While there's no such thing as a "perfect" weight for any one individual, a certain range of calories is needed to maintain health.**

	Age Range	Height	Caloric Intake Range
Males	11-14	5'2"	2700/2100-3900
	15-18	5'9"	2800/2100-3900
	19-22	5'10"	2900/2500-3300
	23-50	5'10"	2700/2300-3100
Females	11-14	5'2'	2200/1500-3000
	15-18	5'4"	2100/1200-3000
	19-22	5'4"	2100/1700-2500
	23-50	5'4"	2000/1600-2400

(Baker and Henry, p. 44)

2. What are the differences between "ideal body weight," "target weight," and "critical weight"?

"Ideal body weight" refers to the weight (or weight range of about 5-10 pounds) of someone your age, gender, and body frame under "normal" circumstances (non-eating disordered). The term "target weight" refers to whatever weight is 95% of your ideal body weight; "critical weight" is 80% or less of your ideal body weight. Generally speaking, if you are at or below critical weight, you should be hospitalized because you are at risk for major, potentially irreversible, physical damage to your body. One of the goals of sustained recovery is to reach and maintain your target weight.

3. What is a setpoint?

Everyone's body has a *setpoint*, which is the weight (again, this is more accurately a weight *range*) that your body tries to maintain no matter how many calories you add or subtract. This weight range is the one at which your body is working most efficiently and is therefore most healthy.

Your setpoint weight is determined by genetic factors which are not changeable, and by your metabolic rate, which is explained in #4 below. Any daily food intake below 1200 calories for two weeks or more lowers the setpoint, as does keeping your weight less than your setpoint range. When this happens, all chemical reactions in your body slow down; your muscle tone, body temperature, and blood sugar levels decrease; and the ability of your heart muscle to work declines to 50% of its previous rate per minute. The longer you diet/restrict, the longer it will take for your body to normalize and its setpoint to return to normal.

4. What is metabolism (metabolic rate)?

Metabolism is the rate at which your body burns calories. Partial or total starvation is a physiological stress, which the body reacts to by automatically slowing down its metabolic rate. Metabolism fluctuates on a regular, 24-hour cycle: it tends to be slowest upon awakening in the morning and gradually increases to a peak around dinner time. Then it slows gradually. When you sleep it reaches that lowest point. *Metabolic rate increases during and after exercising and, ironically, after eating.* Also, certain medical conditions or medications can affect your metabolism, but we're not addressing these exceptions to the rule here.

5. What are Body Mass Index, BMI, and BMI-for-age?

Body mass index (BMI) is a measurement used by physicians and dietitians to determine if the amount of fat in your body is appropriate and adequate to sustain your physical health. BMI increases as you grow into adulthood. BMI is calculated by the following equation: **weight** *(in pounds) divided by* **height** *(in inches) squared multiplied by* **703**. Many websites will do the math for you, one of which is *www.cdc.gov/nccdphp/dnpa/bmi/bmi-adult-formula.htm.*

This measurement applies differently to children and teens than it does to adults. In children and teens it is referred to as "BMI-for-age" and assesses underweight, overweight, and risk for overweight. It is gender and age-specific. (You can read more about this online at *www.cdc.gov/nccdphp/dnpa/bmi/bmi-for-age.htm*). The BMI for adults is usually used to assess obesity. However, your appropriate BMI-for-age will be determined by your doctor and dietitian. It will then be one of the gauges used by your dietitian to adjust your food plan throughout your recovery.

6. What is involved in initial weight restoration?

Adequate body weight is essential for health—both lean and fat mass protect your vital organs, which is why weight is first regained in the areas of the stomach, buttocks, and back. Muscle weighs more than fat—75% of muscle is water—and in the early stages of recovery the weight gained is comprised of a higher proportion of water and muscle tissue. Since the body wants to rehydrate, and fluid retention will occur because of hormonal changes and the sodium in food, some of the weight you gain is probably due to a fluid shift.

This is important to understand because it's possible to misperceive the physical sensation of fluid retention as out-of-control weight gain, and escalate it into anxiety, obsessive thinking, even panic. You may insist you can "see" a weight gain of one or two pounds on your body, but that's virtually impossible. Fluid retention is *not* an accurate reflection of how "fat" you are (even if "fat" is how you say you feel). Your dietitian will help you learn ways to address and challenge this misperception.

7. What is the Food Pyramid and how can it help me decide on a balanced diet?

The *Food Pyramid* is a guideline for healthful eating from the U.S. Department of Agriculture:

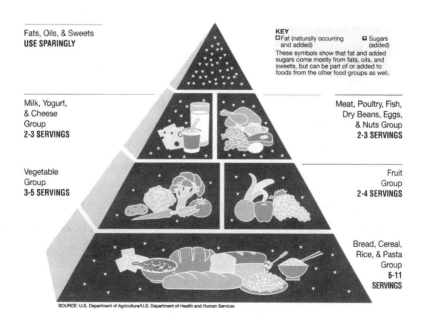

Source: U.S. Department of Agriculture/U.S. Department of Health and Human Services

A balanced diet has

- 60% - 70% carbohydrates

- 12% - 15% protein

- 25% - 30% fat, with no more than 10% saturated fat.

The food pyramid breaks the percentages down and gives you choices:

Milk, Yogurt, Cheese Group
One serving = 1 cup milk or yogurt; 1 1/2 ounces of natural cheese or 2 ounces of processed cheese

Meat, Poultry, Fish, Dry Beans, Eggs, Nuts Group
One serving = 2-3 ounces of cooked lean meat, poultry, fish. 1/2 cup of cooked dry beans, 1 egg, or 2 tablespoons of peanut butter count as one ounce of lean meat.

Vegetable Group
One serving = 1 cup of raw leafy vegetables, 1/2 cup of other veggies cooked or chopped raw, or 3/4 cup of vegetable juice.

Fruit Group
One serving = 1 medium apple, banana, orange, or 1/2 cup of chopped, cooked or canned fruit, or 3/4 cup of juice.

Bread, Cereal, Rice, and Pasta Group
One serving = 1 slice of bread, 1 ounce of ready-to-eat cereal, or 1/2 cup of cooked cereal, rice, pasta.

You should try to eat *at least* the lowest number of servings from the five major food groups listed here. Eating the minimum supplies about 1600 calories; the midrange supplies about 2200; the upper range about 2800. You can find the entire pamphlet on the USDA website: *www.usda.gov/cnpp/pyrabklt.pdf.*

There are other food pyramids as well that focus on different cultural eating patterns. One is the Mediterranean pyramid, which emphasizes consumption of carbohydrates, fresh fruits and vegetables, beans, legumes, nuts, olive oil, cheese and yogurt. Ask your dietitian about this strategy or read about it on the web at *www.oldwayspt.org/pyramids/med/p_med.html.*

8. What are "food exchanges" and why will they make it easier to stick with a food plan?

Food exchanges are just that: exchanges. Many items in your food plan can be substituted for others with similar nutritional and caloric values, so you can honor your food preferences without allowing the prior eating-disordered thinking and behaving to come into play. Since the goal is to normalize your eating patterns gradually and safely, these exchanges help you add variety to a food plan without losing nutritional punch. For instance, if you hate milk but are supposed to drink it, you can exchange it for soymilk. If you must eat bread but don't like it, eat a taco or tortilla instead; if you can't stand red meat, a serving of canned tuna or salmon would suffice, and so on. Your dietitian will teach you how to calculate food exchanges so you get the right proportion of nutrients and the appropriate number of calories. You'll also learn "tricks" to help you determine what a serving of food looks like; for example, a medium size fruit is like a tennis ball or fist, a half cup serving is about the size of the palm of your hand, one ounce of cheese is the size of your thumb, an ounce of nuts is one handful, etc.

9. What is a nutritional supplement and how do I know if it's safe?

A *nutritional supplement* is usually something specific that your dietitian or doctor tells you to include in your food plan to augment missing nutrients, such as a can of *Ensure* or *Boost*, a protein bar, a daily calcium chew, or a multivitamin.

Unfortunately, there are many *unsafe* items marketed as "supplements" that claim to enhance your mood and physical health. For example, kava (to relax you) and St. John's Wort (an antidote for stress, the blues, and depression), popular herbal remedies in the last decade, have now been deemed harmful; kava has been taken off the market. Ephedra has been banned by the F.D.A. but it was recently used in a variety of herbal concoctions. *Do not use anything that contains ephedra.* And don't take a supplement that hasn't been suggested and/or approved by a member of your treatment team.

Nutrition and healthy eating are goals that seem elusive when you are in the throes of an eating disorder. But once you challenge your inaccurate beliefs about the relationship between your food intake and your body's reactions to the foods you select, recovery becomes plausible and probable.

Ten Things to Remember About Nutrition Therapy

1. The nutrition therapy intake usually occurs within a week of your initial therapy interviews.

2. When you are in nutrition therapy, you are expected to talk about food and eating, whereas you may be asked to focus *less* upon food and eating when you are with the other members of your treatment team.

3. The dietitian/nutritionist sometimes focuses on issues and patterns that other therapists also address.

4. The dietitian/nutritionist listens to you with a different "ear" and approaches your problems from a different angle than the other therapists.

5. Nutrition therapy teaches you about the impact of both adequate and inadequate nutrition on your body.

6. Nutrition therapy helps you replace inaccurate beliefs and food fears with correct facts and proper strategies for recovery.

7. Learning nutrition facts, including the meaning of "calorie," "BMI," "setpoint," "metabolic rate," will be part of your nutrition therapy.

8. You and your nutritionist will create a food plan with which you are comfortable. This can be revised as you progress in recovery.

9. You will learn what to do to maintain your health once your body is nourished and you are no longer eating and thinking in an eating-disordered way.

10. There are times when you won't want to believe that what you are being told is best for you. Try to believe that it is.

chapter eleven

Sustaining Recovery

"Recovery is all of these thing: a good brain that thinks clearly, being comfortable in your own body, healthy thoughts about food, no need for symptoms, being able to learn from the past and know how much wiser you now are. Recovery is the hardest thing you'll ever have to do—a lifetime journey. You know how in movies they make this big trek to the top of some mountain and endure all sorts of hardships and finally reach the top overlooking the beautiful valley with trees and lakes and stuff? That's recovery."

– Therapy group consensus, participants ages 14-24

If a group of people in various stages of recovery from eating disorders get together, two questions inevitably arise: "What is recovery?" and "How do you plan on sustaining your recovery?" But another question, often unstated, underlies both of them and is probably the most vital: "Is sustained recovery *really* possible?" The answer is "Yes." Eventually, you'll believe it, even if you're skeptical right now.

So what exactly are we talking about? Sustained recovery stands upon a foundation of knowledge which you've acquired from various sources, including reading books, doing written exercises like those in this book, writing in a journal, talking with your therapy team and others who support your recovery, and making an effort to try out new thoughts and behaviors.

This investigation has armed you with crucial information. You know how *your* particular disorder has impacted your life. You are aware of the changes you've made thus far and why they've been successful. And now, you have the courage and skills to review and revise the changes as necessary so that you can continue to do well and prevent a major relapse.

> **At this point, you are probably prepared for more specific things that you can do to sustain your recovery.**

You can always continue to practice some of the "First Steps" you took in Chapter 6, such as setting goals on a regular basis and avoiding negative triggers. But there's so much more you can do to keep learning about yourself and to understand your disorder once that initial base of competence is in place. Your perspective can and will become a bit broader: you can look back at things that didn't make sense and see precisely why you needed to do or think them in the past but don't need to continue them any more.

Specific Strategies for Sustaining Recovery

Revisit your personal inventory.

Once recovery gathers momentum, it's a good idea to take stock of where you've been relative to where you are now. One excellent way to do this and gauge your progress is to reread your journal and/or your answers to the written exercises in this book. While your day-to-day activities and thoughts might not seem to be changing dramatically, by looking back over a period of weeks or months you'll see how far you've come. You may be surprised and startled by the self-awareness contained in those pages, and how much you've grown as a person. You might even have some "Aha!" moments when all the puzzle pieces seem to fit into a coherent pattern and your direction seems clear.

Choose supportive people and situations.

Although this has been mentioned as an important "first" step in recovery, it remains important throughout the process and is worth repeating. As best you can, try to hang out with people who are supportive of your recovery, and avoid situations or people that trigger your disorder. In practical terms, this might mean *not* hanging out with a crowd of kids whose pastimes and passions revolve around diet, exercise, and weight loss. (Similarly, it's not wise to take a job in a food-related business: waiting tables, short-order cooking, catering, delivering pizzas, and dishing out ice cream might be problematic for you.)

Work on your communication skills.

When you're in the "sustaining recovery" phase, it's crucial that you continue to communicate *accurately* and *adequately* without distorting the content and intent of the conversation. Keep in mind that although communication is a two-way street, sometimes *you* have to be the person who initiates the conversation.

Speak up and clarify your position when you want to say something, whether it is positive, negative or neutral. When you get into the habit of being upfront about your thoughts and feelings, you won't need to use an eating disorder as a way to avoid communication or as a substitute for it.

Also, pay attention to how you're interpreting things that are said *to* you. If you've learned to be alert to your past "scripts" and assumptions, now you'll be able to make sure that what you *think* you're hearing is what the speaker really means to convey. Take a deep breath before you jump to negative conclusions about a conversation. Remember that it's okay to change a response if you find your initial impulse was wrong. Be willing to acknowledge when you've made a mistake and give yourself permission to change your mind *and* your reaction.

Be aware of your thinking processes.

If you sometimes misinterpret what people were actually saying to you, chances are it is because you are making one or more "cognitive errors" (also called "cognitive distortions"), which are "mistakes" in the way you think. Some common goofs are:

- Over-generalizing: making up a general, universal rule from an isolated statement or event;

- global labeling: using negative labels to describe yourself instead of accurately describing your qualities;

- filtering: selectively focusing on the negatives and disregarding the positives;

- polarizing (also known as black and white thinking): thinking something is either perfect or it's worthless, or good or bad with no room for anything in between;

- self-blame: blaming yourself for things that may not really be your fault;

- personalizing: assuming everything has something to do with you as well as negatively comparing yourself to others;

- mind reading: thinking you know what someone else is thinking and feeling, not checking to see which, if any, of your assumptions are true, and presuming their thoughts about you are negative;

- control fallacy: believing you're totally responsible for people and events in your life.

• emotional reasoning: assuming things are really the way you feel about them.

A more complete discussion of cognitive distortions can be found in *Self Esteem* by McKay and Fanning (pp. 65-66).

If you can't completely avoid the habit of reacting based on these errors, at least be alert to them and give yourself permission to change your mind (and response) when you do. That's a start. For instance, you'll be able to stop the recurrence of prior problems or issues that might suck you back into the old ways of "thinking and doing." You'll know how to communicate your positions and interpret others' viewpoints without making the kinds of cognitive errors that used to trip you up. You'll be willing to challenge your eating disordered "scripts" so inappropriate and negative thinking won't resurface and ambush you. Finally, you'll know how to short-circuit any new "issue" from turning into a full-blown problem that might eventually trigger a relapse.

"Stop, think, and regroup" is how one of my patients summarized the cognitive skills she utilized to sustain her recovery and prevent relapse.

> For me, the best way to extinguish the "eating disorder fire" is to reframe the old elementary school adage, "Stop, Drop, and Roll" to "Stop, Think, and Regroup." I first STOP my racing thoughts as well as whatever I'm doing in the actual moment when I'm caught up in anxiety or an eating disorder urge. After I calm down, I listen to myself, THINK a bit, process where my thoughts are coming from and the direction they're heading. Then I try to REGROUP and decide what activity will pull me from the initial impulse. The challenge, of course, is to initiate stop!
>
> – Christie C., age 21

Feel your feelings. Don't numb them.

As a former client said, "Confidence doesn't come from feeding insecurities. It comes from feeding yourself so you can feel those feelings and then challenge and change them if you need to." Eating disorders can be used as a way to divert your attention from deeply held feelings, to numb yourself, or put yourself in physical pain so you ignore the underlying emotion and concentrate on the more obvious physical feelings that result from starvation or bingeing and purging. But once you know how to shift the focus and *really allow yourself to feel the feelings*, the eating-disordered activities are no longer needed and can be eliminated, gradually.

Empower yourself by helping others.

Allow yourself to experience your ability to make a difference in the lives of others, feel good about what you do, and see positive results of your efforts. Do volunteer work. Get a job that is fulfilling, perhaps one in which you work with others as a "team." Join a YMCA leadership club and train to be a mentor. Babysit for the children of working parents after school. Visit an elderly neighbor on a regular basis. Being appreciated by other people raises your self-confidence and helps you appreciate yourself for reasons other than those relating to weight and shape.

Continue to challenge cultural influences that contribute to the epidemic of eating disorders.

Be alert to the hype and bias of anyone and anything connecting self-worth to low weight. Become an attentive TV watcher and magazine reader. Challenge the position of friends who advocate dieting (or are dieting) if you're comfortable doing so. Perhaps explain to them that this is a serious issue. Agree to disagree. Take a stand and say, "No!" to the marketers, advertisers, and media figures who perpetuate impossible beauty ideals. Not only will your attitude change, but the chances are also good that your change will positively affect others!

Make time for playtime and relaxation.

People who have eating disorders don't often know the meaning of being "appropriately selfish" and tend to put their own needs and wants far down their lists of priorities and "to-dos." If you're going to let go of an eating disorder, you must put something else in its place. That is where your hobbies and interests can be effective. Figure out what *you* like to do (not what you think you *should* like, or what you think someone *else* wants you to like) and try to find a balance between work and play. Perfectionism can't be allowed to enter the picture: eliminate the word "perfect" from your vocabulary. The simplest relaxation techniques such as taking a bath, going out for a walk, listening to soothing music, stroking your pet, lighting incense and candles in your room and reading quietly can help, as can more skill-based techniques such as yoga.

Dump the scale!

A scale is not your best friend! Don't keep one in your room or bathroom and don't let yourself sneak a peek if you find one anywhere else. Focus on your renewed, internal connection with your body: how it works, how it feels, and how you feel "inside your skin" as you recover. Don't use a number on your scale as your source of self-esteem.

Be smart about style and size.

Although you are spending a lot of time learning and changing who you are on the inside, how you look on the outside can also help you feel positive about yourself and boost your self-confidence.

Wear clothes that fit well and comfortably. Buy only what you're going to wear *now*. Give away the clothes that represented "success" in your eating-disordered mindset. And *don't focus on the size itself*: manufacturers are inconsistent in sizing, and a zero or a two this year may have been labeled a four or six a few years before. Size is about marketing, and marketing is about money. It really has nothing to do with your self-worth.

Investigate holistic or alternative therapies and/or bodywork.

Many people find that adding a nontraditional, holistic element to their more traditional therapy is an effective tool for sustaining recovery. Yoga, Pilates, and other systems of body movement dovetail with the "expressive therapies" discussed earlier that are usually part of a treatment-oriented environment. Massage enhances body awareness, too, and some forms of body and energy work, such as Cranio-sacral and Reiki, will frequently help a person release deeply-felt emotions.

Even faith healers or psychics have been known to enhance the work done in more traditional therapies. Therapist and author, Thomas Moore, speaking about "Spirituality and Psychology: Healing Body, Soul, and World" at the 19th Annual Cape Cod Summer Symposia (June, 2002), discussed tarot cards as a therapy tool to help clients access their imaginations, tap into emotions, and plumb deeper levels of their personal stories en route to self-awareness.

As long as nontraditional methods don't jeopardize you mentally or physically, they can be antidotes to feeling stuck, enhance your sense of power and *appropriate* control, tweak your beliefs, and provide an extra "push" to sustain your recovery.

Explore your spirituality.

You may find many missing pieces of your recovery puzzle by adding a spiritual component to your recovery. This might be as simple as taking quiet time to think about yourself and the meaning of your life or talking to others about their spiritual lives. Or, it might entail reading inspirational books or the Bible, revisiting the religious path of your family or searching for a path of your own.

Share what you've learned, teach others what you know.

Wanting to share something personal with another individual or group of people is not only a powerful indicator that recovery is happening, but also a way to fortify that recovery. When you feel at ease being open and taking the initiative to say, "I just wanted to let you know . . . " the odds that you can sustain your recovery will increase dramatically and you'll be able to prevent reruns of the old tapes and scripts.

Self-help Groups

Another great way to strengthen your recovery process outside the treatment setting is to attend self-help (support) groups. These can be found on college campuses, as adjuncts to in-patient or out-patient therapy programs, as informal groups of people in varying stages of recovery, or as components of existing Overeaters Anonymous programs, and so on. Self-help groups meet in a variety of settings, including rented space at local churches, hospitals, or members' homes. Typically, participants include people who are in recovery from some form of eating disorder (and perhaps additional psychological or addictive challenges) and their families or friends.

Self-help groups vary dramatically in the ways in which they are run. A trained professional may sit in, but doesn't necessarily lead the group; responsibility for the group's tone and tempo remains with the participants. The therapist's role in that context is as a backup in case of emergency or crisis.

If you choose to attend a self-help group, understand that although it's a great addendum to therapy, it's *not* a replacement for professional help.

Self-help groups are free or charge a minimal membership fee, publish monthly newsletters, and often have hotlines for you to call when you're feeling disheartened. Sometimes groups function as stable and reliable social networks, but they aren't meant to be a place to find romantic partners. Many self-help groups (for example, Alcoholics Anonymous) discourage private interpersonal contact until the person is free of the disorder or addictive behavior for at least a year.

It might surprise you that many people with anorexia and bulimia attend meetings of Overeaters Anonymous (OA), an organization founded in 1960 for compulsive overeaters and patterned after the twelve-step program of Alcoholics Anonymous (AA). Some bulimics find OA's strict requirements comforting and helpful: you limit yourself to three meals a day, restrict your range of foods at mealtime, avoid sugar and other binge-triggering substances, check in with your sponsor daily by phone, and attend weekly, even daily, OA meetings. Others find this system triggering because it seems to increase an inappropriate focus on food and may escalate the desire to binge. How you respond to a self-help strategy is personal. Not liking one doesn't mean there's something wrong with you or that the program is bad; it just means you must keep searching until you find a group that "fits" your needs and wants.

Buddy-system Support

Buddy-system support networks can also be effective support for your ongoing recovery. Typically, your therapist will put you in touch with other of his or her clients who are willing to be your phone partners. They will talk to you when you need to connect with someone who has "been there, done that." A phone buddy can help you through a crisis in the moment, applaud you when you've made a breakthrough (and lean on you to applaud yourself), or listen with an objective ear in way that a more intimate friend or relative might be unable to do. Ideally, this buddy will reach out to you as well, and together you can hone your communication skills, catch one another in cognitive distortion modes, be alert to signs that either of you is in an eating disorder "zone" and not be dissuaded by protests to the contrary.

Since each buddy is working with the same therapist, you're familiar with the format and "jargon" of the process, so you automatically speak a similar language of healing. Buddy-system support networks are frequently composed of the same people you may know from a group therapy situation, or they may be individuals you've never met and don't plan to meet in person. Either way, the decision to reveal your full name is a personal choice. The therapist is simply the go-between and only provides a first name and phone number. The rest is up to you.

Help via the Computer

Although much of your recovery has probably been supported by therapists, doctors, and other in-person individuals, sometimes you might want to gather information on your own or talk to someone anonymously. That's when a computer with Internet access can be an ally. There are a variety of online websites that function like virtual reference librarians. Some are maintained by organizations dedicated to education about and prevention of eating disorders. Here is a partial list:

- AED (Academy for Eating Disorders) *www.aedweb.org*

- ANAD (National Association of Anorexia Nervosa & Associated Disorders) *www.ANAD.org*

- Gürze Eating Disorders Resource Catalogue *www.bulimia.com*

- IAEDP (International Association of Eating Disorders Professionals) *www.iaedp.com*

- NEDA (National Eating Disorders Association) *www.nationaleatingdisorders.org*

- Pale Reflections Eating Disorders Community *www.pale-reflections.com*

- The Renfrew Center Foundation
  www.renfrew.org
- Something Fishy Website on Eating Disorders
  www.something-fishy.org

These sites are among the most respected in the eating disorders field, and the information they contain can be relied upon to be accurate and ethical. But you must use Internet resources intelligently. If you question the truthfulness of something you read elsewhere, check several sources to see if their information is basically the same. Be alert to discrepancies and discuss them with your primary support people.

Online chat rooms, bulletin boards, and *email* can also be useful additions to your recovery strategies and function a lot like cheerleaders and "reality checkers." Since most schools and public libraries have computer terminals and since there are many free email sites, anyone with access to a computer can utilize these resources.

Chat Rooms

If you're feeling isolated, down, or scared, or if you need a diversion, want to defuse the urge to binge and/or purge, or need reassurance about trying to eat or having eaten, a chat room is a "place" you can go anytime. They operate around the clock, and some online services have special-interest chat rooms for members. Some "feel" like a casual social gathering, while others operate more formally, with regularly scheduled meetings or pre-selected discussion topics. Various chat rooms have "regulars" who frequent the sites so often people know one another well, and members can be alert to the depth and seriousness of each other's problems. The regulars can be guides or mentors to new participants, and sometimes serve as crisis managers. It's also possible to create private chat rooms and wait for people who share your interests to arrive and talk.

Chat rooms offer anonymity, so you can vent safely, without embarrassment. An online experience can be useful when you're hesitant to otherwise admit you're struggling, wavering, wondering about the value of recovery, and/or feel like you're about to resume the eating disordered behaviors. It can be a place to defuse the tension of sustaining recovery without undoing what's necessary to stay free of the restricting, bingeing, or purging.

> **As with anything else pertaining to the Internet, you must be cautious in chat rooms.**

Anonymity can make it easy for other people to lie about themselves. Never reveal personal information that could allow a stranger to locate you.

That said, *chat rooms do provide a sense of community*. Online groups are sometimes the only way for people who are already in therapy to meet others like them because they live in areas of the country in which eating disorder support groups are unavailable. Strong emotional bonds can be formed and much encouragement and wisdom can be shared online.

Chat rooms also enhance perspective. For those of you who are in the midst of your recovery, chat room conversation offers a mirror in which to check and reflect upon your progress and accelerate your commitment to recovery. Sometimes the visual impact of words scrolling on your computer monitor literally can make you "see" things differently or help you connect with your own ambivalence about the difficulty of recovery and the value of getting well. If you are about to take the plunge into a more aggressive attempt at recovery, a chat room can provide the impetus to do so.

A chat room discussion gives you the chance to be a mentor. If you are long recovered, dropping into a chat room from time to time can help you keep your resolve to remain free of your eating disorder. You will undoubtedly be a source of inspiration and wisdom for someone in that room. On the other side of the coin, because of the anonymity factor, it's relatively easy to ask for advice from others in the online community who have assumed the role of mentors.

A chat room can be like a continuing education course open to anyone. People who aren't eating disordered may drop in and ask questions or simply "listen" to the conversational drift. Because a chat room is interactive, it provides a very different experience than that of reading a book or article about any eating disorder or going to a specific website for factual information. Chatting with strangers can be less draining and more focused, direct, and honest than talking "in real life" with people you know; online discussion can yield insights that might not have otherwise happened.

Bulletin Boards

Bulletin boards are just what the name implies — places for people to tack up virtual notes to which others can respond. In general, each bulletin board has regulations, similar to a code of ethics, for posting and responding. The Pale Reflections website, for example, rates the bulletin board postings according to their potential for triggering someone's eating-disordered thinking and behaving. As with chat rooms, the rule of thumb is that you access the bulletin board to communicate with others who share your focus or interest; privacy and confidentiality are not possible.

Email

Email gives you the opportunity to write directly from your email address to anyone else who has an email address. The instant intimacy of email can be a powerful incentive to "tell all" or to ask questions you don't have courage to discuss openly and in person. Sometimes it's just a way to connect and vent, an immediate release that helps you block and redirect eating-disordered thinking and behaving. In any case, be cautious and remember the relationship is a "virtual" one. "What you see is what you get" may not apply.

Many professional organizations and therapists in the field of eating disorders are willing to be contacted by email. Most of the sites listed in the Website section (pgs. 196-7) have registers of licensed professionals. Realize, however, that if you make the contact and ask for advice, that person cannot and will not advise you as if responding in the capacity of your therapist unless you then hire them to function in that role.

The Challenge of Participating in Athletics

Many individuals with eating disorders are athletes who have spent much of their time focused on the connections between (and importance of) peak physical shape and optimal performance. Often, physical activity is severely restricted in the early stages of treatment for anorexia or bulimia. A sure sign of recovery is when you're told you can resume whatever sport or physical, athletic activity that used to be part of your daily life. While that can be exhilarating on the one hand, it also poses a series of challenges.

If you think about the qualities that make someone a successful athlete, they include:

- the ability to focus on a goal and make a commitment to it,
- the willingness to practice,
- the diligence needed to hone physical skills,
- the tendency to push physical limits to some extremes,
- a shift from self-focus into team-focus even if it means you must "squelch" your individual voice,
- close attention to the coach's authority.

These very qualities can trip you up and make sustained recovery difficult unless you take some steps to avoid being sucked back into the patterns and beliefs of your prior athletic history that supported your eating disorder.

1. *Don't buy into the myths and inaccurate beliefs about sports performance*: that someone who appears to be in "good physical shape"

is in excellent physical health (not necessarily true); that weight loss is equivalent to fat loss (not true); that lower fat intake improves athletic performance (it doesn't); or that not having a period (amenorrhea) is normal and a desirable consequence of training (it isn't).

2. *Be aware of "the female athlete triad," which refers to three linked conditions, eating disorders, amenorrhea (absence of menstruation), and osteoporosis (bone loss), associated with athletic training* (especially gymnastics, figure skating, ballet, distance running, diving, swimming, cheerleading). The demands these sports make on your body are often contrary to what that body would do and how it would look if nature were allowed to take its course. Make a vow to yourself and assert, "I won't do anything related to the physical demands of my sport that would put me back in this triad."

3. *Realize that you have the right to question and challenge any coach or mentor who encourages behaviors that would jeopardize your health.* Excessive exercise, restricting, purging should never be required or made to seem "normal." Just because an adult authority figure says that something has to be a certain way does not necessarily make it right. An arbitrary number that appears on a scale or a weight-height chart should not dictate your lifestyle, self-image, or self-esteem, and should *never* be a reason for your physical health to suffer.

Sustained recovery is both your right and your responsibility. Its form and function will change over time, and eventually it will become second nature to you to live your life without the constant hum and background noise of an eating disorder. Just remember that recovery doesn't follow a linear path, and there will be times when the eating disorder will try to resurface. If and when it does, it's trying to alert you to something important. Pay attention to what's going on, and then use your hard-won skills to challenge and block its recurrence.

Ten Things to Help You Sustain Recovery

1. Remember that the state of recovery is fluid: it ebbs and flows, and rarely progresses in a straight line.

2. Give yourself permission to look at the past and share what you've learned with others, but avoid shame, blame, or guilt.

3. Take stock of why you've been successful in your recovery thus far, so you can feel confident when your recovery goals and strategies need revision.

4. When you "stop, think, and regroup" before reacting, you can prevent recurrences of the old, eating-disordered ways.

5. Sustained recovery is based on accurate communication patterns rather than distorted ones.

6. You don't need to numb your feelings or let the eating disorder do your talking for you any more.

7. Use of internet resources can help you fight off the tendency to isolate yourself.

8. Once you're allowed to resume athletic activity, you'll have the skills to challenge myths and inaccurate beliefs about sports performance that previously triggered your eating-disordered behaviors.

9. Relaxation is part of recovery—give yourself the luxury of occasional inactivity.

10. Don't take someone else's words at face value without careful consideration of what seems appropriate for you and your health.

chapter twelve

Helping Someone Who Has an Eating Disorder

"If I knew then what I know now, I'd say to anyone embarking on the recovery journey that you need patience, trust, faith, luck, a lot of humor, and the absolute belief that you are going to succeed, even if it is in a way you never expected."

— Mrs. H., mother of a 16-year-old anorexic daughter

It's a natural and commendable impulse to want to help someone you care about work through a problem. When that person is struggling with anorexia or bulimia, your own skill and attitude are keys to successful results. You'll have to draw upon your knowledge of eating disorders, be aware of the limits of your effectiveness, and pick the right time to intervene.

In spite of your best efforts and good intentions, it's inevitable that your hard work won't always have the impact you'd intended, and you should be prepared to be misunderstood and even rebuffed if your help is either unappreciated or unwanted. However, it's just as likely that your support, love, and concern will have a powerful and positive influence. The challenge is to remember the latter when you're faced with the former.

The Challenge of Helping

The principal reason why your good intentions may be misread is that individuals with eating disorders develop abnormal habits and beliefs that interfere with interpersonal relationships. Caring may be misinterpreted as coercion. Compliments may be felt as performance pressure. Attempts at discussion may be misconstrued as accusations. Your honesty may be heard as distortion of facts. What you say or do might be attributed to jealousy of the eating-disordered person or your need to control the situation. Your attempts to see humor in the situation (and there *is* humor) might be perceived as trivializing the person's struggle and the significance of the eating disorder. Not only can reactions such as these be frustrating, they can cut off communication at the outset if you are not aware that they are more typical than atypical.

Here are some examples of communication attempts gone awry.

If my parents say, "Can you come here? We want to talk to you," my stomach still clenches. From past experiences I know it means intense, difficult conversations that no one wants. So now, "Can you come here? We want to talk to you," is a signal that they'll talk at me and I'll cry. But every time I've said this to my mom and dad, they deny it and tell me I'm imagining things and that they are just doing what my therapist asked them to do, which is, of course, talk. Talk has so many meanings, doesn't it?

My mom makes it seem like I've failed when she asks me how I'm doing. Could I do better? Of course I could. She should just tell me she's upset that I'm not perfect. She's used to me picking up concepts really quickly and getting things accomplished really fast. Recovery doesn't work that way.

My mom will throw out comments like, "What did I do wrong?" or "I never meant to mess you up like that." She says, "We should have been able to stop it." Then she'll add, "I'll do anything you want—what can I do to help?" and I think, "Yeah, right. Anything." I don't believe her. I feel like she's passing the guilt off onto me.

She was talking to me as if she really wanted to be my friend. But then she said, "Sometimes I need a daughter," and I didn't understand why she said that. I didn't understand how I'm not being a daughter. I couldn't hear a thing after that because I froze. I felt so attacked.

Can you hear the frustration in the voices of these people? Do you see how the apparent inability to trust each other affects their ability to *accurately* hear what's being said and interpret what's being offered? Do you see how someone in "helping mode" can inadvertently become entangled in a no-win situation that leads to hurt feelings?

Fortunately, there are ways to overcome these negative interactions, and, with practice, avoid them altogether. If you're direct, willing to state your opinions and explain what's going on inside your head, *agree to disagree,* and acknowledge that hurt feelings are normal during such an intensely emotional time, you'll be more apt to put misunderstanding aside and be able to move forward. Everyone must be willing to try again and again until communication flows smoothly and your trust base is unshakeable. Although it's easier said than done, it is definitely possible.

Deciding What You Expect to Accomplish by Helping

"Help" can be a loaded term. It may mean one thing to you and something entirely different to the object of your attention. Your role will vary depending on your relationship with the person, the severity of the eating disorder, the level and intensity of ongoing therapy, and how much energy you choose to expend. It's important, at the outset, to develop personal definitions of "helping" and "helper" that will include *your* specific goals and projected timetable for meeting them.

Start by answering a difficult question: "Why do I want to help this person?" Be honest. Are you *truly* doing this as a gesture of your concern and affection for the other person, or are you trying to score points with the family or your mutual social circle? If it's to score points, stop now because you could create more problems than you're trying to solve.

Don't get involved if you believe you will gain control over the other person and "teach her (him) a lesson" for the pain the eating disorder has caused everybody. Helping is not about "one-upmanship" or righting wrongs.

Are you doing this primarily to alleviate your own fright, discomfort, anxiety, and/or anger about the eating disorder's impact on everyone's lives? If so and your reactions are that intense, first clarify them.

> **You may need some short-term counseling to give you a safe place to express yourself.**

Then, if and when your own needs are addressed, you can proceed as a helper and be a much more reliable source of support.

Six Rules to Make You an Effective and Appreciated Helper

One of the best things you can do to make yourself an effective and appreciated helper is to develop a base of knowledge and skill. Don't worry if this process makes you feel like you need a Ph.D. in "Helping" to do what seems like a natural act.

Rule #1: Be informed.

Learn as much as you can about eating disorders before you offer help of any kind. Reading this book and others, searching the web for information, and talking to other people (professional or otherwise) who have experience with eating disorders are all ways to build an accurate knowledge base and become aware of the complexities inherent in recovering from anorexia and bulimia. It's also important to be on-target when you evaluate the seriousness of the problem and anticipate arguments the other person might use to prove you wrong.

Rule #2: Make sure there really is a problem.

If you *know* there is a problem, make sure it's is what you think it is. Avoid assumptions! When in doubt, ask the person. As obvious as this rule seems, it's easily forgotten.

> *I noticed scars on my girlfriend's knuckles soon after we started dating and I knew she'd been going to the dentist a lot lately, so I made the assumption that she was a bulimic. That's when I found out a little knowledge could be a dangerous thing. Instead of asking her point-blank, I kept sneaking in references to bingeing and purging and how bad it was for you. I even looked through her bathroom cabinets for laxatives. I thought I could help her since she liked me so much and we got on so great. But she caught me snooping. She let me have it. Her scars were from an old riding accident and she was going to the dentist to have a crown on her molar repaired. We'll never go out again—she was that mad at me.*
>
> – Randolph M., age 17

We can make many assumptions about what we *think* we see happening (as Randolph did) and offer help based on two premises: that our assessment of the situation is correct (Randolph's wasn't) and that our solutions are workable and constructive. All-too-often, they're not. If this is the case, the best course of action is to admit your mistake. Apologize, apologize, apologize. Explain why your thinking took a wrong turn and how it influenced your behavior. At the very least, make a case for yourself by stating the fact that you are an alert and observant person who honestly believed you were doing the right thing—even though you goofed.

You can avoid mistakes like Randolph's by being direct. If you suspect that someone you know has an eating disorder, talk to her or him before you do anything. You may not get a straight answer, but at least you'll be playing with your cards face-up on the table. That way, you're less likely to be accused of breaching boundaries or behaving inappropriately.

Rule #3: Define the nature of your relationship with the person you want to help.

To do so, answer the following questions:

1. What's your relationship to the person (parent, sibling, friend, teacher, "significant other," spouse, employer)?

2. How long have you known the person?

3. How well do you know the person?

4. In what context do you know the person (home, school, work, leisure situation, place of worship)?

5. How formal is your relationship? (Are you an authority figure such as a parent, teacher, or employer who is more apt to be perceived as a "superior" than as an "equal," or is the relationship equal in terms of power or status? Are you peers in terms of age and life-stage?)

6. What's your normal, everyday communication style with that person? (Do you tend to lecture rather than have a conversation? Are you confidantes, or do you talk openly but not intimately? Do you speak your mind, or do you leave a lot unsaid?)

Obviously, the nature of your relationship will influence how your efforts are received. If you're the parent of someone who is eating disordered, the ordinary stress, strain, and intensity of that parent-child relationship will color and magnify any reactions to your help. Even if you're 100% right, you might be met with more resistance and denial than a non-relative would. If your relationship with the person is more formal than "personal," your efforts may be perceived as coercive or bullying. If you're confidantes, you risk jeopardizing the closeness of the relationship if the person isn't yet ready for help. A more casual acquaintance is apt to be seen as pushy or nosy. If you're the romantic or sexual partner, tact, delicacy, and a heightened degree of understanding are crucial for your helping efforts to be acceptable.

Special Issues for a Romantic Partner to Consider

Let's look at the special issues inherent in helping a romantic partner take the road to recovery. A romantic/sexual relationship is an intense, emotional connection between people who are physically attracted to each other and who discover, over time, that they can trust each other in a special way. That trust makes it possible for them to share their innermost thoughts without fear of ridicule or exposure, and allows the physical aspects of the attraction to blossom and find expression in a romantic context.

You may hear people say, "Sex is the most natural thing in the world," and it may be, but physical and sexual expression can be excruciatingly difficult for people with eating disorders. Since body-image issues are exaggerated and distortions are commonplace, physical intimacy can be very difficult to achieve and maintain. In fact, it can be frightening. Many young women who have eating disorders will say they feel "fat and ugly" even when they're not. The tendency is to perceive the "self" as body parts, scrutinizing their breasts, stomach, hips, thighs, and buttocks instead of being able to look in a mirror and see the whole person. When a particular woman literally cannot see what her lover sees, humor evaporates, joking is impossible, and trust is replaced with doubt. A silly joke or offhand remark can be absorbed as insulting and scornful.

> *My fiancé came into my mom's living room when I was stretched out on her couch on my stomach. I guess my butt was up in the air, and Howie gave me a pat on it when he tried to sit down. I was horrified. I felt like all my fat must have been visible through my spandex. So then, when he called me his "little whale," I freaked. I haven't even been able to let him see me in a bathing suit since that day! And he just doesn't understand.*
>
> – Flo G., age 20

The special bonds between people who've been romantically linked are often changed when an eating disorder comes into play. So if you're trying to help a girlfriend or partner, you can't *assume* that she'll respond to you as she did before the eating disorder became an issue and/or was acknowledged. Try to remember that because she's insecure about her physical self, she's likely to be insecure about your view of her; she may automatically assume you see her as the imperfect person she feels herself to be. An eating disorder often changes and even replaces communication: once her situation is revealed, your partner may seem guarded and unwilling—even unable—to share the confidences and intimacies that were once so much a part of what made you a couple.

So what do you do? Tell her what you value about her and about yourself when you are with her. (Any reference to "her" can also be applied to "him" if the eating-disordered individual is male.) From time to time, make sure she's hearing you accurately and literally ask her, "What did you hear me say?" Then ask her if she's ready and willing to hear your spin on how the eating disorder has impacted each of you and altered the nature of your relationship. If she says "Yes," tell her how you feel. If it hurts you to see her do this to herself, explain why. If she says she's willing to let you help her, if she's willing to include you in her therapy or to have you help her search for an appropriate resource, and you're ready to be her ally, tell her.

> **Be honest about your hesitations and your fears. If you are relieved and happy that she is allowing you "in," make sure to tell her how much her trust means to you.**

If you don't understand what she's doing, ask questions, but re-assure her that your purpose in asking is self-education, not to place blame, shame, or guilt on her. Take some responsibility for your feel-ings—*own them*. If you become frustrated or find yourself with a short fuse, tell her *in the moment*, and make sure to indicate that your feelings don't mean that you think she's a "bad" person. They simply indicate your level of tension at that point in time. In other words, don't give her a chance to make a cognitive error about you.

Make sure she knows she has both the right and responsibility to tell you to back off if you're moving too fast for her, or it she feels you're breaching a boundary—prying or pressuring. Discuss how she wants to handle socially-oriented eating situations such as going out to dinner with you and other friends. Does she want you to signal her if she looks as if she's about to panic, or if she seems to be verging on a binge right there in the restaurant? Does she want to give you a signal that she needs you to help calm her or help her refocus? If so, what is your response to be? Something as simple as touching your hand and you responding by a hand squeeze may suffice. If you rehearse your roles in advance, some of the anticipatory anxiety will evaporate. Does she want you to watch what she's eating and comment about it, or does she want you to ignore any food-related behaviors? Make sure to revise your strategies over time, as her needs may change dramatically and you don't want to be stuck doing things that are no longer soothing and supportive.

Intimacy issues may be even more difficult than eating issues to discuss. Ease into the topic, respect her heightened sensitivity about her physical self, and *don't bombard her with a list of grievances*. If you find her attractive, tell her as much as you can about what attracts you, and don't let her dwell on "fat issues." If she seems to withdraw from physical intimacy, respect her need for distance and ask her what she would like you to do to help her begin to feel more comfortable within her physical self. If she says "Nothing," respect that and try again another time. If someone is in a self-deprecating mode, she cannot and will not hear anything positive that is said about her and probably will recoil from being emotionally or physically touched. Furthermore, if you persist in trying to break down that physical barrier when she is telling you she can't "go there" with you right then, you risk pushing her further back into the disconnected mindset in which she sees herself as body parts, not as a whole being.

If you are willing to let the relationship continue and evolve during her recovery, it's imperative that you think and talk positively. For instance, point out that the physical, intimate aspects of your relationship could become enhanced as a result of your mutually-increased sensitivities to each other's needs and wants. Or talk about how your emotional commitments to one another could be strengthened because the relationship is chosen over the eating disorder.

> **Remind her how good it feels to ask for and receive unconditional support from another person.**

Rule #4: A person with an eating disorder must want help and be ready to accept help for your efforts to have a positive impact on the situation.

It's often said that, "timing is everything." This bit of folk wisdom applies here. Wanting to be helped and being ready to accept help aren't necessarily the same things, but fall along a continuum of readiness factors determined, in part, by how long the eating disorder has been in place. Remember that anorexic and bulimic behaviors can become obsessions, compulsions, and addictions, and they gain more and more control of their victims the longer they're allowed to persist. So, unless the person has willingly opened up to you first, you can increase your chances of getting a positive response by waiting for the right time.

How do you know when that moment has come? Pay close attention to your dialogues. If you're cautious and respectful, know your limits, pick your battles as you talk together, and really listen to the person's responses, you'll know it's right because conversation flows, there's agreement as well as disagreement, and the tension around the topic eases.

On the other hand, if the person you're trying to help is 5'8", weighs 80 pounds, and wants to lose more weight, or can't eat a meal without vomiting immediately afterward, or has to engage in a minimum of five planned binge-purge episodes, he or she won't be able to hear your words of caution, logic, and concern. That person will "defend" the eating disorder and thwart your challenges. Statements such as the ones that follow make loud and clear the fact that there is still a lot of emotional energy invested in the eating disorder and the person is not ready to give it up.

> *The only time I'm really by myself is in the bathroom. It's the only place I'm not judged.*

> *I feel I've never really been allowed to change things in my family. I live in a dictatorship, not a democracy. My eating disorder is my only haven.*

It gives me power over how I look to myself. It's like I'm in control—I can choose what I want to do with my eating habits. No one can take it away from me. It's all mine. You can't force me to do it. It's my choice.

If this is the case, your efforts to help may be appreciated by the person's family and friends, but not by the individual with the eating disorder at that point in time. Leave major challenges about the eating disorder to a professional who is trained to help people reframe entrenched attitudes and beliefs. However, if you understand the limits of your helping role and still want to proceed, go ahead and tell that person what you're willing to do and how long you're planning to stick around. Be prepared to be thwarted, nonetheless, and have a plan of action for bowing out gracefully if you must. This leads directly to the next rule.

Rule #5: Understand and accept that there may be times when you can't help, regardless of your good intentions and knowledge.

Few things feel as terrible as being rejected by someone to whom you've reached out, no matter how prepared you are for that possibility. Your phone calls are refused. If you stop by for a visit, no one will answer the door, or you'll be told the person is unavailable. You might get the silent treatment if you try to talk face-to-face. Your emails or IMs ("Instant Messages" if you're online at the same time) will be ignored or blocked.

Don't automatically assume these reactions are due to something that you've done wrong. They are more likely to be an indication that the eating disorder has too strong a hold on the person and professional intervention is needed. Or, they may mark a transitional phase when the eating disorder is becoming more severe and occupying more of the person's "head space." They may be a response to feeling intense pressure to get well from outside sources (i.e., *you*), but the person hasn't reached the point of "recovery readiness." Also, as mentioned before, an eating disorder often functions as a barrier that excludes not only people who have previously been significant (and you may fall into that category), but things such as interests and hobbies.

So, even if the person's reason for rejecting your help isn't apparent, but the clear message is, "Go away, leave me alone, get lost!" you must respect it. Everyone must learn this rule, even the professionals on the treatment team. Their knowledge and expertise do not give them the power to help someone who doesn't want it, and there are no guarantees that what works with one person will work for all.

Every helper takes emotional risks and must be prepared for rejection. Remember that there's always the chance that your currently unsuccessful attempts at helping will eventually pay off—when you least expect it, the person might tell you that she or he is ready to accept your help and thank you for your previous efforts!

> **You may find out that what you've done has actually been a source of relief and that you forced the issue at the right time.**

You might be the person whose input plants the seed of recovery, making it a possibility and even a probability.

It's also okay to want to give up. There's only so much one person can do for another, and we all have limits to how patient we can be and how much frustration and rebuffing we can tolerate.

I was 15 and I felt like I had to save Janys, that no one else could stick with her, handle her moods, and understand her fixations about her looks. But my grades began to suffer. I began to lose my personality. My other friends got really jealous and annoyed, and they didn't invite me to hang out the way they used to. When Janys and I went out, I got tired of

*never being able to order ice cream or French fries, and hav-
ing to pretend I liked balsamic vinegar and fat-free everything.
I don't—I never have, never will. But most of all, I felt my
energy was gone. I couldn't do it anymore. I had to look out
for myself. I hope that wasn't too selfish. I'll be here for Janys
if she can be more flexible, and I hope her therapy will help
her be a kid again.*

– Brinley D., age 15

Knowing when you've reached your *own* limits of helping and
stopping whatever it is that has brought you to the brink is just as
important to your own health and well-being as is the gesture of
helping someone else retain or regain theirs.

Rule #6: Adjust Your Communication Style

People who have eating disorders usually have a lot of self-doubt.
Many come from backgrounds in which appropriate, productive
communication is lacking or absent. As a result, they often don't
feel comfortable speaking up for themselves or might not think they
have the right to do so. They might not even know *how* to clearly
state their needs and expectations. Even worse, some might have
been punished when they tried, and then stopped altogether. But
needs and expectations don't just "go away" because they're ignored
or repressed. After a long period of time, those unexpressed thoughts
and emotions build up until the pressure becomes so uncomfortable
it has to be released. An eating disorder is often the outlet.

If the person you're trying to help has a similar kind of history,
you should modulate your helping approach accordingly. Try to avoid
being brutally honest or confrontational so you don't accidentally
and unintentionally threaten the person's already unsteady sense of
self. This could make things worse by adding to her anxiety, thus
increasing her need to turn to the eating disorder for safety. To a

person who hasn't developed the skill and habit of speaking up, someone who does might be perceived as inappropriate, pushy, nosy, brazen, threatening, or even nuts!

How can you be honest without being perceived as a threat? Try these tactics:

- Don't act like you're the judge and jury. That's not your job.
- *Never* accuse.
- Be aware of your tone of voice and the possible "bite" of your words; try to hear yourself as the person listening to you might hear you.
- Use "I" language.
- Refrain from using "You" language.

The last two points, which were also mentioned in Chapter 5, are worth repeating. If you say, "I love you and I'm worried about the effect of your eating habits on your health," you are using "I" language. The message is caring and comes from your point of view. Because it belongs to you, the listener can't argue with it.

"You" language, on the other hand, sounds like this: "Your eating habits are killing you, and you're driving me nuts with your behavior. You know how much I love you, so you should understand why I'm getting on your case about this!"

Do you hear the difference? Even though the facts are the same in both, the underlying care and concern of a "You" mesage is buried under what feels like finger-pointing. "You" language statements are accusatory and invite arguments. Responses to the example above could be, "My habits aren't killing me—I'm still alive, aren't I?" "You're already a lunatic," or "If you cared, you'd leave me alone."

There are other things you shouldn't say to someone who has an eating disorder. *Never* say (not even in jest), "I wish I could have anorexia for a week or two" or "I know what you're going through because I have weight concerns/body-image issues/self-esteem problems, too." You *don't* know what it's like to have an eating disorder unless you've been there yourself.

> **Being concerned with weight, self-esteem, or body-image isn't the same as being eating disordered.**

People who joke about being anorexic are probably trying to say that they wish their bodies were thinner. If that's what you want to talk about, say so. However, you should avoid comparisons about body shape or weight since that kind of discussion often triggers a competitive need in the anorexic or bulimic person to "win" at the imagined thinness competition, as we've discussed previously. Don't make an eating disorder seem like a desirable condition, especially to someone who might grasp at any straw to justify continuing that behavior.

Humor can be Healing

Sometimes laughing at the very things that get you down is therapeutic, and in this situation, humor can be a useful tool for you and the person you're trying to help. You can start out by poking gentle fun at yourself for being clumsy in your approach to things. You can mimic how therapists talk. It's plausible that *if* the two of you become comfortable laughing together you'll eventually be able to talk about more difficult issues (the key concept here is "comfortable" because that implies neither of you will be in a defensive posture). If you decide to take the lighthearted approach, be aware of your delivery. What is humorous to you might not be humorous to the other person. Make it clear that you're trying to defuse some tension and *you are not trying to minimize the seriousness of the eating disorder and the suffering it causes.*

You can laugh together about almost anything that pertains to an eating disorder, as long as you both agree that it is okay.

You might find it funny that someone would need to cut a pea into eight pieces; you might marvel at the clothing or food choices people make as they pass through the various stages of recovery. Medical issues like how spacey some medications make you feel, the "eating-disordered voices" inside your head, where people choose to vomit, and so on, can each be observed through a lens that alters the way you each view it. Laughter is meant to help accelerate and support the healing process by putting a different spin on things that might otherwise seem ponderous and frightening. However, *never laugh at the person or say/do anything to mock or demean the struggle to recover from an eating disorder.*

In addition to that universal (and obvious) warning, do not poke fun at issues relating to past or present physical, psychological, or sexual abuse the person you're helping might have experienced, as well as any kind of family dysfunction, such as alcoholism or drug addiction. If the person brings it up and is willing to laugh about them, you can join in, but in general it's better to be respectful and cautious about discussing these problems.

Strategies for the Tenacious Helper

What can you do when you want to stay connected, to prove your caring and commitment, even though you keep getting rebuffed or ignored? Let's assume the rejection isn't a result of anything *you've* done to blow the relationship or cause it irreparable damage—it's clearly because the eating disorder has colored and changed the individual's perception of you. You have faith that your friendship can resume, if not in the exact state it was pre-disorder, at least ready to develop into something as valuable (and perhaps even more prized for having been sustained in spite of this major challenge). You want to stay connected, to prove your commitment to the person. What can you do?

There is a variety of other ways you can communicate that perhaps aren't as threatening as talking one-on-one. A starting point is to write letters talking about anything and everything you want to discuss, knowing they might never be read. If you "snail mail" them, chances are someone will save them unopened until the other person is ready to read them. (You might want to keep copies of each just in case they do get pitched in the garbage by the recipient.) You can use email and keep a backup file of the letters on your computer. Some internet services enable you to see if sent mail has been read or deleted.

Another possibility is to record what your life is like without that person in it. In a diary or journal, write about the events and activities that used to involve both of you and how it feels not to have the other person's company and input. If you and that person worked at the same place or went to the same school, and she or he had to drop out of school or quit work, expand the diary or journal into a scrapbook. Include clips from school newspapers, work memos, photos of friends or colleagues, even silly little things like notes passed in class or socially-oriented "events" announcements at work. Try to keep it current.

If you have access to a video camera, you can create a similar record of life in the person's absence, complete with music, appearances by friends and family, scans of photos, digital images, etc. You can set up a video camera on a tripod and record yourself talking to your friend or relative; don't stop taping even if you find yourself tearful and choked up. Sharing your vulnerability could help the person eventually "risk" an equal degree of honesty and openness with you. You can give the finished product to that person whenever it suits you, and hope it will be accepted. If not, you've tried your best and that is all anyone can expect of you.

Rebuilding Relationships

What about relationships that have been damaged by an eating disorder? Can they be rebuilt or repaired? The answer is a qualified, "Yes." Often, when people with eating disorders get far enough along in recovery, they feel compelled to try to restore relationships that were once important to them. This could happen after they repeatedly rejected your help but you kept trying, or long after you stopped. It often happens after the person has had some professional therapy. The assumption is that since the relationship existed before, it's realistic to think it could exist again.

What should you do? Do you take that person back with open arms even if your ego has been bruised? Do you say, "I forgive you for everything"? Or do you say, "I'll give you one more chance"? When you're in the driver's seat, you have to decide the direction in which you want to go. *Don't* let yourself act on any initial impulse to recount the experience from your point of view and perhaps even play the blame game. There is no place for blame, shame, or guilt in this situation; it won't change the past, it might jeopardize what you're trying to rebuild now, and it could make a future relationship based on trust too hard to sustain.

Instead, clearing the air could be a good place to start rebuilding the relationship. Your timing for when to suggest doing this depends on the stage of the person's recovery. If he or she has just been discharged from an inpatient hospitalization setting, to be able to connect with you at all is a triumph and it would be unrealistic for you to expect to be able to clear the air just then. However, if the person has been in recovery for several months and has a network of support, such as therapy or a self-help group, your request to sit down and talk would be reasonable.

> **No matter what happens,
> treat the other person with respect.**

You're only human; so too, is the person you have tried to help. Whatever may result from your efforts, you will learn a lot about yourself: about your inner resources and what it feels like to give your all for another person. You will have shown love, and that's when we humans are at our best.

If you care about someone who has an eating disorder and want to help, just remember that you have a better chance of succeeding if you have the knowledge base, consider the rules listed in this chapter, and are genuinely concerned about the person's well-being. The payoffs for both of you can be extraordinary, as this excerpt from a letter to me shows:

> *My college roommate had her third bout with anorexia during our freshman year. It was rugged. Because my mom is a therapist, I knew a lot about eating disorders long before I went to college, but I also knew about them because a close girlfriend in high school was bulimic. So you could say that I was a natural for helping. I tried again and again to be supportive of my roommate. I gave her books to read, we wrote gratitude journals together, I'd sit up with her nights listening to her crying because of frustration and self-doubt, I talked to her boyfriend when she was afraid to, and I tried to eat meals with her, though that made me want to scream.*

> *At one point I moved out for a week because I was so frustrated and almost said she was being selfish and self-destructive on purpose. After a while, though, I developed a sixth sense that told me when it was time to stop worrying. I saw little signs like her talking more to me, us laughing together more, noticing that she went to buy groceries and came back home in less than an hour. I also remember the first time she bought a box of animal crackers and the first time she suggested we have a party in our room. Things got better between us, too; both of us relaxed.*

> *Anyway, the week of graduation, she gave me a journal she had kept that included illustrations, photos, and song lyrics that described what I had done for her, what it meant to her, and how I changed her life. It's funny, you know? She changed mine, too. As hard as it was, I wouldn't have missed that experience. It gave me such a strong sense of the power of commitment and cooperation, selflessness, and, yes, of love.*

> *– Shelby H., age 22*

Ten Things for Helpers to Remember

1. Be informed and avoid assumptions about the person and the disorder.

2. Be certain about your answers to, "What am I trying to accomplish as a helper?" and "What's in it for me?"

3. Make sure each of you understands and agrees to one another's definitions of "helping" and "helper."

4. Your helping role will vary depending on the severity of the eating disorder, the time frame of recovery, the level and intensity of therapy, and the nature of your relationship to the person.

5. Helping is *not* about getting even, teaching a lesson, taking control, one-upsmanship, or righting wrongs.

6. Any helper will sometimes be rebuffed (or worse).

7. Your caring may be misinterpreted as coercion, conversation heard as accusation, compliments experienced as performance pressure.

8. Romantic partners as helpers face special challenges because of the ways in which eating disorders impact intimacy issues.

9. If you're cautious, respectful, know your limits, pick your discussion topics (and battles) appropriately, you'll be able to determine when it's time to step in as a helper and when it's time to back off.

10. Try to hear yourself as the person you're helping might hear you.

Freedom

by Lindsay N.G., age 17

*It's peculiar the way the light can reflect when a fresh morning
dawns within you.*

*A blinding display, a brilliant array of acute and vibrant aware-
ness*

*flooding the soul, filling the cracks of isolation with the dew-
drops of self acceptance.*

*The night finally at bay when one can declare her conflicted
place no longer conflicted;*

*eyes once held at half mast are blown open by gradually grow-
ing winds of true vision.*

*A dove sings a song of harmony that flows through a body no
longer in bondage.*

*What a shame it would be never to know the freedom that comes
with the morning.*

Definitions of Eating Disorders

Many health care professionals use the *Diagnostic and Statistical Manual of Mental Disorders* (published by the American Psychiatric Association) to help them correctly diagnose their clients' problems. This is how the most recent edition, the *DSM-IV-TR,* describes some of the varieties of eating disorders:

Anorexia Nervosa:

A. Refusal to maintain body weight at or above a minimally normal weight for age and height (e.g., weight loss leading to maintenance of body weight less than 85% of that expected; or failure to make expected weight gain during period of growth, leading to body weight less than 85% of that expected).

B. Intense fear of gaining weight or becoming fat, even though underweight.

C. Disturbance in the way in which one's body weight or shape is experienced, undue influence of body weight or shape on self-evaluation, or denial of the seriousness of the current low body weight.

D. In postmenarcheal females, amenorrhea, ie., the absence of at least three consecutive menstrual cycles. (A woman is considered to have amenorrhea if her periods occur only following hormone, e.g., estrogen, administration.)

Specify type:

Restricting Type: during the current episode of Anorexia Nervosa, the person has not regularly engaged in binge-eating or purging behavior (i.e., self-induced vomiting or the misuse of laxatives, diuretics, or enemas).

Binge-Eating/Purging Type: during the current episode of Anorexia Nervosa, the person has regularly engaged in binge-eating or purging behavior (i.e., self-induced vomiting or the misuse of laxatives, diuretics, or enemas).

Bulimia Nervosa:

A. Recurrent episodes of binge eating. An episode of binge eating is characterized by both of the following:

(i.) eating, in a discrete period of time (e.g., within any two-hour period), an amount of food that is definitely larger than most people would eat during a similar period of time and under similar circumstances

(ii.) a sense of lack of control over eating during the episode (e.g., a feeling that one cannot stop eating or control what or how much one is eating)

B. Recurrent inappropriate compensatory behavior in order to prevent weight gain, such as self-induced vomiting; misuse of laxatives, diuretics, enemas, or other medications; fasting; or excessive exercise.

C. The binge eating and inappropriate compensatory behaviors both occur, on average, at least twice a week for three months.

D. Self-evaluation is unduly influenced by body shape and weight.

E. The disturbance does not occur exclusively during episodes of Anorexia Nervosa.

Specify type:

Purging Type: during the current episode of Bulimia Nervosa, the person has regularly engaged in self-induced vomiting or the misuse of laxatives, diuretics, or enemas.

Nonpurging Type: during the current episode of Bulimia Nervosa, the person has used other inappropriate compensatory behaviors, such as fasting or excessive exercise but has not regularly engaged in self-induced vomiting or the misuse of laxatives, diuretics, or enemas.

Eating Disorder Not Otherwise Specified:

1.   For females, all of the criteria for Anorexia Nervosa are met except that the individual has regular menses.

2.   All of the criteria for Anorexia Nervosa are met except that, despite significant weight loss, the individual's current weight is in the normal range.

3.   All the criteria for Bulimia Nervosa are met except that the binge eating and inappropriate compensatory mechanisms occur at a frequency of less than twice a week or for a duration of less than three months.

4.   The regular use of inappropriate compensatory behavior by an individual of normal body weight after eating small amounts of food (e.g., self-induced vomiting after the consumption of two cookies).

5.   Repeatedly chewing and spitting out, but not swallowing, large amounts of food.

Binge-eating disorder: recurrent episodes of binge eating in the absence of the regular use of inappropriate compensatory behaviors characteristic of Bulimia Nervosa.

Suggested Reading and Sources Cited

The following list includes both references from the text of *The Beginner's Guide*, as well as titles of my "favorite" books that I recommend for further reading. Each one is coded according to its most appropriate audience.

P = Professional reader

G = General reader

T = Teen or college-age reader

American Psychiatric Association (Editor), *American Psychiatric Association Practice Guideline for the Treatment of Patients With Eating Disorders, Second Edition.* Washington, D.C.: American Psychiatric Press, Inc., 2000. P

Anderson, Arnold, Leigh Cohn and Thomas Holbrook. *Men's Conflicts with Food, Weight, Shape & Appearance.* Carlsbad, CA: Gürze Books, 2000. G

Baker, Susan, and Robert R. Henry. *Parents' Guide to Nutrition.* Reading, MA: Addison-Wesley, 1986. G

Blinder, Barton J., et al. *The Eating Disorders: Medical and Psychological Bases of Diagnosis and Treatment.* New York: PMA Publishing Corp., 1988. P

Bordo, Susan. *Unbearable Weight: Feminism, Western Culture, and the Body.* Berkeley, CA: University of California Press, 2003. G

Brown, Lyn M., and Carol Gilligan. *Meeting at the Crossroads: Women's Psychology and Girls' Development.* Cambridge, MA: Harvard University Press, 1992. G/T

Brownell, Kelly D., and John P. Foreyt, eds. *Handbook of Eating Disorders: Physiology, Psychology, and Treatment of Obesity, Anorexia, and Bulimia.* New York: Basic Books, 1986. P

Bruch, Hilde. *Conversations with Anorexics.* New York: Basic Books, 1998. G/T

ibid., The Golden Cage: The Enigma of Anorexia Nervosa. Cambridge, MA: Harvard University Press, 1978. P/G/T

Brumberg, Joan Jacobs. *The Body Project: An Intimate History of American Girls.* New York: Random House, 1997. G/T

Cash, Thomas F. *The Body Image Workbook: An 8-Step Program for Learning to Like Your Looks*. Oakland, CA: New Harbinger Publications, Inc., 1997. G/T

Cash, Thomas F., and Thomas Pruzinsky, eds. *Body Image: A Handbook of Theory, Research, and Clinical Practice*. New York: The Guilford Press, 2002. P

Chernin, Kim. *The Hungry Self: Women, Eating, and Identity*. New York: Times Books, 1985. G

ibid., *The Obsession: Reflections on the Tyranny of Slenderness*. New York: Harper & Row, 1981. G

ibid., *Reinventing Eve: Modern Woman in Search of Herself*. New York: Harper Perennial, 1987. G

Cooke, Kaz. *Real Gorgeous. The Truth about Body & Beauty*. New York: W.W. Norton & Company, 1996. G

Costin, Carolyn. *The Eating Disorder Sourcebook: A Comprehensive Guide to the Causes, Treatments, and Prevention of Eating Disorders*. Los Angeles, CA: Lowell House, 1997. P

DePalma, Mary T. et al. 1993. "Weight Control Practices of Lightweight Football Players." *Medicine and Science in Sports and Exercise* 25. mp/ 6:694-701. P

Ellis, Albert. *Anger: How To Live With and Without It*. New York: Citadel/ Kensington Publishing Corp., 1997. G/T

Emmett, Steven W., ed. *Theory and Treatment of Anorexia Nervosa and Bulimia*. New York: Brunner/Mazel, 1985. P

Empfield, Maureen and Nicholas Bakalar. *Understanding Teenage Depression: A Guide to Diagnosis, Treatment, and Management*. New York: Henry Holt and Company, 2001. P

Fairburn, Christopher. *Overcoming Binge Eating*. New York: Guilford, 1995. G

Fairburn, Christopher, and G. T. Wilson. *Binge Eating: Nature, Assessment, and Treatment*. New York: Guilford Press, 1993. P

Fallon, Patricia, Melanie A. Katzman, Susan C. Wooley, eds. *Feminist Perspectives on Eating Disorders*. New York: Guilford Press, 1994. P

Fodor, Viola. *Desperately Seeking Self*. Carlsbad, CA: Gürze Books, 1997. T

Foehrenback, Lenore, and Robert Lane. 1989. "Bulimia — Its Dynamics and Treatment: The Case of an Adolescent Male." *Journal of Contemporary Psychotherapy* 1, no. 3: 183-201. P

Freedman, Rita. *Bodylove: Learning to Like Our Looks & Ourselves*. Carlsbad, CA: Gürze Books, 2002. G/T

Gaesser, Glenn A. *Big Fat Lies: The Truth about Your Weight and Your Health*. Carlsbad, CA: Gürze Books, 2002. P/T

Garfinkel, Paul E., and David M. Garner. *Anorexia Nervosa: A Multidimensional Perspective*. New York: Bruner/Mazel, 1982. P

Garner, D. M., and P. E. Garfinkel. 1979. "The Eating Attitudes Test: An Index of Symptoms of Anorexia Nervosa." *Psychological Medicine* 9:278. P/G/T

ibid., eds. *Handbook of Psychotherapy for Anorexia Nervosa and Bulimia*. New York: Guilford Press, 1985. P

Gayle, Lisa. 1997. "Eating Disorders and Our Children." www.family.com/features/family_1997_03/metp199703_eating/. G

Gentry, W. Doyle. *Anger-Free: Ten Basic Steps to Managing Your Anger*, New York: Quill, 1999. G/T

Ginsburg, Lynn and Mary Taylor. *What Are You Hungry For?* New York: St. Martin's Griffin, 2002. G/T

Gottlieb, Lori. *Stick Figure: A Diary of My Former Self*. New York: Penguin Putnam, Inc., 2000. T

Hall, Lindsey and Leigh Cohn. *Bulimia: A Guide to Recovery, Fifth Edition*. Carlsbad, CA: Gürze Books, 1999. T

Hall, Lindsey and Monika Ostroff. *Anorexia Nervosa: A Guide to Recovery*. Carlsbad, CA: Gürze Books, 1999. T

Hirschmann, Jane R., and Carol H. Munter. *When Women Stop Hating their Bodies*. New York: Fawcett Columbine, 1995. G

Hornbacher, Marya. *Wasted: A Memoir of Anorexia and Bulimia*. New York: Harper Flamingo, 1998. G/T

Jack, Dana C. *Silencing the Self: Women and Depression*. Cambridge, MA: Harvard University Press, 1991. G

Johnson, Carol A. *Self-Esteem Comes in All Sizes: How to Be Happy and Healthy at Your Natural Weight*. Carlsbad, CA: Gürze Books, 2001. G/T

Johnson, Craig, and Pauline Powers. 1996. "Eating Disorders and Athletes: An Exciting Development in Prevention." *The Renfrew Perspective* 2-1 (spring). P

Johnston, Anita. *Eating in the Light of the Moon: How Women Can Transform Their Relationships With Food Through Myths, Metaphors & Storytelling.* Carlsbad, CA: Gürze, 2000. G

Kaye, Walter H., and Harry E. Gwirtsman. *A Comprehensive Approach to the Treatment of Normal Weight Bulimia.* Washington, DC: American Psychological Association Press, 1985. P

Kilbourne, Jean. *Can't Buy My Love: How Advertising Changes the Way We Think and Feel.* New York: Touchstone, 1999. G/T

Lachenmeyer, J. L., et al. 1988. "Laxative Abuse for Weight Control in Adolescents." *International Journal of Eating Disorders* 7, no. 6 (Nov): 849-52. P

Lask, Bryan, and Rachel Bryant-Waugh, eds. *Anorexia Nervosa and Related Eating Disorders in Childhood and Adolescence.* UK: Psychology Press, 2000. P

Levenkron, Steven. *Anatomy of Anorexia.* New York: W.W. Norton, 2000. G

ibid., *The Best Little Girl in the World.* New York: Warner, 1978. T

ibid., *Kessa.* New York: Basic Books, 1986. T

ibid., *The Luckiest Girl in the World.* New York: Penguin Books, 1997. T

ibid., *Obsessive-Compulsive Disorders: Treating and Understanding Crippling Habits.* New York: Warner, 1991. G

Maine, Margo. *Body Wars: Making Peace with Women's Bodies.* Carlsbad, CA: Gürze Books, 2000. G

ibid., *Father Hunger: Fathers, Daughters, and Food.* Carlsbad, CA: Gürze Books, 1991. G/T

McKay, Matthew and Patrick Fanning. *Self-Esteem: A Proven Program of Cognitive Techniques for Assessing, Improving, and Maintaining Your Self-Esteem.* Oakland, CA: New Harbinger Publications, Inc., 1992. G

Mehler, Philip S. 1996. "Eating Disorders: 1. Anorexia Nervosa." *Hospital Practice* (January 15). P

ibid., "Eating Disorders: 2. Bulimia Nervosa." *Hospital Practice* (February 15). P

Mellin, Laurel M., et al. 1992. "Prevalence of Disordered Eating in Girls: A Survey of Middle-class Children." *Journal of the American Dietetic Association* 92: 851-53. P

Minuchin, Salvador, et al. *Psychosomatic Families: Anorexia Nervosa in Context.* Cambridge, MA: Harvard University Press, 1978. P

Mondimore, Francis Mark. *Adolescent Depression: A Guide for Parents.* Baltimore: The Johns Hopkins University Press, 2002. G

Normandi, Carol Emery, and Laurelee Roark. , *It's Not About Food: Change Your Mind, Change Your Life, End Your Obsession With Food and Weight.* New York: A Perigee Book, 1998. G/T

ibid., Over It: A Teen's Guide to Getting Beyond Obsessions With Food & Weight. Novato, CA: New World, 2001. T

Olivardia, Roberto, and Harrison Pope et al. 1995. "Eating Disorders in College Men." *American Journal of Psychiatry* 152: 1279-85. P

Orbach, Susie. *Fat Is a Feminist Issue, revised.* New York: Berkley, 1994. G

ibid., Fat Is a Feminist Issue II: A Program to Conquer Compulsive Eating. New York: Berkley, 1982. G

ibid., Hunger Strike: The Anorectic's Struggle as a Metaphor for Our Age. New York: Norton, 1986. G

Otis, Carol L., and Roger Goldingay. *The Athletic Woman's Survival Guide: How to Win the Battle Against Eating Disorders, Amenorrhea, and Osteoporosis.* Champaign, IL: Human Kinetics, 2000. G/T

Pipher, Mary. *Hunger Pains.* New York: Ballantine Books, 1995. G/T

ibid., Reviving Ophelia. New York: Random House, 1994. G

Rabinor, Judith Ruskay. *A Starving Madness: Tales of Hunger, Hope & Healing in Psychotherapy.* Carlsbad, CA: Gürze Books, 2002. G

Rodin, Judith. *Body Traps: Breaking the Binds That Keep You from Feeling Good About Your Body.* New York: Quill/William Morrow, 1992. G/T

Roth, Geneen. *Appetites: On the Search for True Nourishment.* New York: Dutton, 1996. G

ibid., When Food Is Love: Exploring the Relationship Between Eating and Intimacy. New York: Dutton, 1991. G

ibid., When You Eat at the Refrigerator, Pull Up a Chair. New York: Hyperion, 1998. G

Sark. *Inspiration Sandwich: Stories to Inspire Our Creative Freedom*. Berkeley, CA: Celestial Arts, 1992. T

ibid., Transformation Soup: Healing for the Splendidly Imperfect. New York: Fireside, 2000. T

Seligman, Martin E. P. *Authentic Happiness: Using the New Positive Psychology to Realize Your Potential for Lasting Fulfillment*. New York: Free Press, 2002. G

Sigler, Jamie-Lynn and Sheryl Berk. *Wise Girl*. New York: Pocket Books, 2002. T

Smolak, Linda, and Michael Levine. 1994. "Toward an Empirical Basis for Primary Prevention of Eating Problems with Elementary School Children." *Eating Disorders: Journal of Treatment and Prevention* 4: 293-307. P

Steenland, Sally. 1995. "Barbie and the 'Deadly Cult of Thinness.'" *Stamford Advocate* (June 9): A13. G/T

Striegel-Moore, Ruth H. and Linda Smolak, eds. *Eating Disorders: Innovative Directions in Research and Practice*. Washington, D.C.: American Psychological Association, 2001. P

Strober, Michael, ed. *The International Journal of Eating Disorders*. New York: Wiley Periodicals, Inc. This journal is an official publication of the Academy for Eating Disorders and is online at www.interscience.wiley.com. P

Ussery, Lydia W., and Steven Prentice-Dunn. 1992. "Personality Predictors of Bulimic Behavior and Attitudes in Males." *Journal of Clinical Psychology* 48, no. 6 (November): 722-28. P

Williamson, Donald A. *Assessment of Eating Disorders: Obesity, Anorexia, and Bulimia Nervosa*. New York: Pergamon Press, 1990. P

Wolf, Naomi. *The Beauty Myth: How Images of Beauty Are Used Against Women*. New York: William Morrow, 1991. G/T

Zerbe, Kathryn J. *The Body Betrayed: Women, Eating Disorders, and Treatment*. Washington, D.C.: American Psychiatric Press, Inc., 1993. P

Index

About the Author

Nancy J. Kolodny, M.A., M.S.W., L.C.S.W., has worked in the field of eating disorders for over 20 years as a therapist, writer, speaker and client advocate. Her areas of specialization are the prevention and treatment of eating problems and disorders, phase-of-life issues, and the challenges of family dynamics. Her book, *When Food's a Foe,* was released in three editions (Little Brown '87, '92 & '98) and was chosen by Booklist as a Young Adult Nonfiction "Editor's Choice" for 1988. She also coauthored *Smart Choices: A Guide to Surviving at Home and in School, Dating and Sex, Dealing with Crises, Applying to College, and More* (Little Brown '86) and *How to Survive Your Adolescent's Adolescence* (Little Brown '84) which was selected as a resource by the National PTA and The March of Dimes, and by CBS Educational and Community Services. Kolodny has developed and implemented educational programs and workshops within both the public and private sectors, has served as a media consultant, and has appeared on television and radio in connection with her books. She has a private practice in Norwalk, CT., is listed in several "Who's Who" volumes and is the mother of three adult daughters.

Nancy Kolodny may be contacted by email with questions, comments, or suggestions about this book at: NJKolodny@aol.com.

About the Publisher

Since 1980, Gürze Books has specialized in quality information on eating disorders recovery, research, education, advocacy, and prevention. Gürze publishes books in this field, as well as the *Eating Disorders Today*, a newsletter for individuals in recovery and their loved-ones and *Eating Disorders Review,* a clinical newsletter for professionals. They also widely distribute free copies of *The Eating Disorders Resource Catalogue,* which includes listings of books, tapes, and other information. Their website (*www.bulimia.com*) is an excellent internet gateway to treatment facilities, associations, basic facts, and other eating disorders sites.

Order at www.bulimia.com
or by phone (800)756-7533

The Beginner's Guide to Eating Disorders Recovery is available at bookstores and libraries or may be ordered directly from the Gürze Books website, *www.bulimia.com*, or by phone (800)756-7533.

FREE Catalogue

The Eating Disorders Resource Catalogue has books on eating disorders and related topics, including body-image, size-acceptance, self-esteem, and more. It is a valuable resource that includes listings of non-profit associations and treatment facilities, and it is handed out by therapists, educators, and other health care professionals throughout the world.

www.bulimia.com

Go to this site for additional resources, including many free articles, hundreds of eating disorders books, and links to organizations, treatment facilities, and other websites. Gürze Books has specialized in eating disorders publications and education since 1980.

Eating Disorders Today
A newsletter for individuals in recovery and their loved-ones

This compassionate and supportive newsletter combines helpful facts and self-help advice from respected experts in the field of eating disorders. Request a sample issue!